EDITOR: MARTIN WINDROW

MEN-AT-ARMS SERIES 43

OSPREY MILITARY

NAPOLEON'S GERMAN ALLIES 2 NASSAU & OLDENBURG

Text by
OTTO VON PIVKA
Colour plates by
G A EMBLETON

D1474397

First published in Great Britain in 1976 by
Osprey, an imprint of Reed Consumer Books Ltd.
Michelin House, 81 Fulham Road,
London SW3 6RB
and Auckland, Melbourne, Singapore and Toronto

ISNB 0 85045 255 4

Filmset in Great Britain
Printed through World Print Ltd, Hong Kong

The Organization of Nassau's Troops 1806-1815

In 1806 Nassau consisted of twin duchies – Nassau–Usingen and Nassau–Weilburg. These lands were the rump of the ducal possessions which existed up to that point; those lands on the west bank of the Rhine and many of those on the east bank having been taken by France or by the newly founded Grand Duchy of Berg (see *Napoleon's German Allies (I)* in this series). Among the lost provinces were Nassau–Saarbrucken and Nassau–Oranien. As compensation for these losses, Prince Friedrich Wilhelm of Nassau–Weilburg received the districts of Limburg and Ehrenbreitstein (opposite Koblenz on the Rhine–Moselle junction). It was traditional under the old Holy Roman Empire of German Nations that the various states of Nassau banded together to provide part of the infantry regiment known as the 'Oberrheinisches Kreisregiment' together with the troops of the micro-states Hohenzollern–Sigmaringen, Hohenzollern–Hechingen, Isenburg, Lichtenstein and von der Leyen.

Prince Carl Wilhelm of Nassau–Usingen was compensated for his territorial losses by part of the lands of the old Electorate of Mainz including the districts of Königstein, Cronenberg, Höchst, Hochheim, Castel, Eltville and Rüdesheim, the old Cologne Electorate districts of Linz and Deutz, and the old Hessen–Kassel district of Braubach. These new territories each brought with them smaller or larger bodies of troops of varying states of efficiency and the composition of the four infantry battalions which the united houses of Nassau now (1803) raised was as follows:

Nassau–Usingen
    1st (Leib) Bataillon: Based on one old company in Wiesbaden.
    4th Bataillon: Based on one old company in Biebrich. These two battalions became the 1st Nassau Infanterie-Regiment in May 1808.

Baron Conrad Rudolph von Schäffer, major-general and commander of the Nassau brigade in Spain. (This portrait shows uniform of a lieutenant-general in the army of the Grand Duchy of Baden, to which service he transferred in 1813.) Of Swedish extraction, von Schäffer was born at Hagen–Osen, Hanover, in 1770. In 1784 he served in the 10th Hanoverian Cavalry (Prince of Wales's Light Dragoons), transferring to the service of Mainz in 1799, as a captain in the newly-raised Jägerkorps. This unit was taken into the service of Nassau–Usingen in 1802 and von Schäffer retained his then rank of major. The unit became the 3rd (Jäger) Battalion of Nassau's tiny army. On 28 May 1804 he was promoted lieutenant-colonel, taking command of the Nassau brigade; rising to colonel on 17 September 1806, he distinguished himself in the campaign against Prussia of that year. On 5 January 1807 he received the cross of the Legion of Honour, and a year later was promoted brigadier-general. In 1808–9 he fought in Spain and held various staff appointments under Marshal Lefébvre. He was invalided home to Nassau, handing over command of the brigade to von Kruse and taking an appointment in the war department after his recovery. He retired in 1833 and died in 1838. The Baden uniform illustrated is dark blue faced red with gold buttons and embroidery.

Nassau–Weilburg
> *2nd Bataillon:* Garrisoned in Weilburg.
> *3rd (Jäger) Bataillon:* Garrisoned in Deutz and Linz.

Each infantry battalion had two three-pounder 'regimental cannon'. In May 1808 these two battalions became the 2nd Nassau Infanterie-Regiment. There was also a company of garrison troops in the Marxburg fortress.

On 17 May 1803 Fürst (Prince) Friedrich August succeeded to the throne of Nassau–Usingen and when, on 16 July 1806, the houses of Nassau joined Napoleon's Confederation of the Rhine, Friedrich August became Herzog (Duke) of Nassau and Fürst Friedrich Wilhelm of Nassau–Weilburg was confirmed as Prince of Nassau. Friedrich August was thus head of state of Nassau and he was charged, under the terms of the treaty of the Confederation of the Rhine, with co-ordinating and organising the military efforts

of all the tiny states previously mentioned as well as those of Frankfurt, Aremberg and Salm. This remained a pious hope, however; Frankfurt remained independent until 1866 and Aremberg and Salm until 1810, when they were incorporated into Metropolitan France.

One unit was newly raised at the time of the 1804 reorganisation of Nassau's lands; this was a regiment of *Jäger zu Pferde* (mounted rifles or Chasseurs à Cheval) also often referred to as the '*Reitende Jäger*'. The bases for this unit were tiny groups of 'Hussars' (really a type of police force) from the old territories of Nassau–Usingen, Wildenburg and Hachenburg, and some men of the Austrian cuirassier regiment 'Nassau–Weilburg' of which the Fürst of Nassau–Weilburg was colonel-in-chief (Chef). Initial strength was one company and their commander was Rittmeister Johann Heinrich Ludwig von Bismark, late of Hanoverian and Mainz service. In 1807 Napoleon

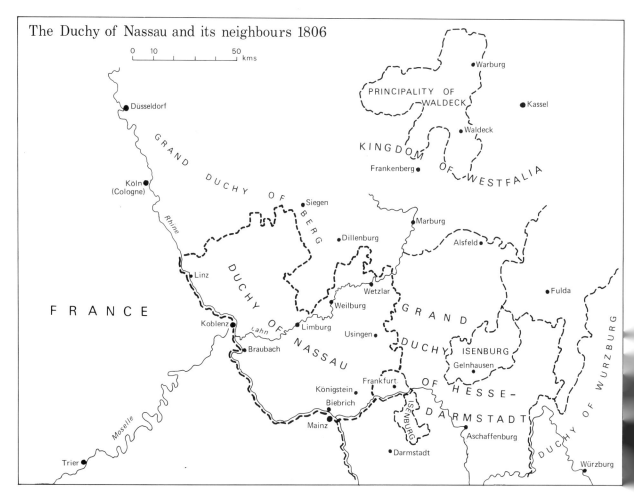

The Duchy of Nassau and its neighbours 1806

battalions raised in 1803 had four companies each of four platoons which again divided into two sections. A company was commanded by a captain (Hauptmann) and had three officers and 137 men; the whole battalion had fifteen officers and 563 men. Line of battle was two ranks deep, the tallest men being on the flanks, the smallest in the middle. Recruiting was by a type of conscription and by the enlistment of volunteers. In March 1808 each battalion was reorganised into five companies. The second reorganisation of July 1808 produced two infantry regiments each of two battalions each of one grenadier, four fusilier and one voltigeur company.

The new 1st Regiment was commanded by

Major-General August von Kruse. Born at Wiesbaden, Nassau in 1779, he entered the service of Hanover as a foot guard officer in 1796. In July 1803, as a lieutenant, he transferred to Nassau–Weilburg and on promotion to captain took command of the Weilburg infantry battalion, later the 2nd Battalion of Nassau's 1806 contingent. By October 1806 he was a major; he fought well in that year's Prussian campaign and in September 1807 rose to lieutenant-colonel. For the Spanish campaign he organised and commanded the 2nd Nassau Infantry Regiment, which took part in no less than 42 battles and skirmishes in the Peninsular War. Promotion to colonel came in December 1808, and he led the brigade after von Schäffer's departure due to illness. In November 1813, acting on secret orders from the Duke of Nassau, he took his regiment over to the British and was repatriated to Germany. On 22 August 1814 he at last achieved major-general's rank but in 1815 the intended re-unification of Nassau's two infantry regiments was frustrated by the speed of military events and von Kruse took a position on Wellington's staff. He retired from Nassau's military service in 1837 and died in January 1848. His decorations included the Grand Cross with Diamonds of the Imperial Russian Order of St Anne, the Legion of Honour, Nassau's silver Waterloo Medal, and the insignia of a Knight of the Royal Netherlands Military Willems-Order.

Major-General Georg Alefeld. His dark green uniform with black velvet facings bears gold epaulettes and embroidery, and the decorations include the Royal Netherlands Military Willems-Order 4th Class, the Waterloo Medal, and the 25 years' service medal. Alefeld was born in 1789 in the Rhineland Palatinate, and was commissioned an officer in the Hessen–Kassel Infantry Regiment 'Kürfurst' in October 1804; with Napoleon's dissolution of this state in 1806 he entered Nassau service as a second lieutenant in von Kruse's 2nd Battalion. After fighting in the 1806 campaign he transferred in spring 1809 to the 1st Nassau Infantry Regiment where, as a lieutenant, he took part in the campaign against Austria before marching to Spain. On 22 March 1810 he was wounded at the capture of the powder-mills of Manresa; later that year, promoted captain, he took command of the 1st Grenadier Company. After his regiment was disarmed by the French in Barcelona on 22 December 1813 he escaped and made his way home. He fought at Waterloo, and later commanded the 2nd Nassau Infantry Regiment. He retired in 1850 and died at Wiesbaden in July 1856.

demanded that a light cavalry regiment be raised as part of Nassau's contingent for the Confederation of the Rhine and the *Reitende Jäger* were expanded into a regiment of two squadrons.

Drill, discipline and distinctions of rank of these new forces were after the Austrian model which was introduced on 7 June 1803, but in 1810 these all gave way to the then current French army regulations and rank badges. Each of the four

5

Oberst von Pöllnitz and consisted of: the grenadier company and three fusilier companies of the old 1st Battalion, and the light company and one fusilier company of the old 4th Battalion. The remainder of the regiment was made up with new recruits.

The new 2nd Regiment was commanded by Oberstleutnant von Kruse and consisted of: the old 2nd Battalion (1 grenadier and 4 fusilier companies); the old 3rd Battalion (1 light and 4 fusilier companies); one fusilier company of the old 1st Battalion; and one fusilier company of the old 4th Battalion.

On 20 August 1808 the 2nd Regiment marched off for Spain where its losses were so high that two more companies of the old 4th Battalion had to be sent off as reinforcements before the end of the year. The 1st Regiment now absorbed the contingents of Isenburg (291 men) and the two houses of Hohenzollern (193 men for Sigmaringen and 97 men for Hechingen). Aremberg, Salm, Lichtenstein and von der Leyen paid a subsidy to Nassau who then raised the required manpower for them.

This military constellation of two infantry regiments and a light cavalry regiment was retained until November 1813 when the two rulers of Nassau left the Confederation of the Rhine and joined the Allies against Napoleon. The 1st Infantry Regiment and the *Reitende Jäger* were disarmed and interned in Spain by the French; the 2nd Infantry Regiment went over to the British and was repatriated to Nassau.

In the upsurge of German nationalism which bloomed in 1813 Nassau raised a 3rd Infantry Regiment, a Landwehr Infantry Regiment (Territorial volunteers) a Jäger Corps and a twenty-nine battalion strong Landsturm or Home Guard. The 3rd Infantry Regiment was commanded by Oberst von Steuben, the Jäger Corps by Oberst von Winzingerode. These two regiments and the Landwehr Infantry Regiment formed a brigade commanded by Oberst von Bismarck.

In June 1814, after the end of hostilities, the Landwehr Regiment and the Jäger Corps were disbanded, the 3rd Regiment was reduced to a company and combined into the depot of the old 1st Regiment. The *Reitende Jäger* were not reraised.

With the collapse of the Confederation of the Rhine in 1813 the old principality of Nassau–Oranien was recreated and an Infantry Regiment of Nassau–Oranien of two battalions and a Jäger Company under Oberstleutnant von Schaffner was formed. The Jäger company was attached to Oberst von Winzingerode's Jäger Corps, the infantry regiment operated with the Nassau brigade and in 1815 was in Dutch service.

The Duchy of Oldenburg in the Napoleonic Wars

By a fortunate mixture of clever diplomacy and luck, Herzog Peter Friedrich Ludwig of Oldenburg managed to keep his duchy out of the wars of 1805 and 1806. Napoleon pursuaded him to join the Confederation of the Rhine by the Treaty of Erfurt on 14 October 1808. The military contingent to be maintained by the duchy was set at an infantry battalion of 800 men in six companies (one grenadier, four fusilier and one voltigeur). On 13 December 1810 Napoleon abolished the Kingdom of Holland, the Duchy of Oldenburg, the old imperial cities of Hamburg, Bremen and Lübeck and combined them (and parts of the old Electorate of Hanover, the Grand Duchy of Berg, the Kingdom of Westfalia and the Duchy of Ahremberg) into Metropolitan France.

THE RUSSIAN CAMPAIGN 1812

On 28 February 1811 (the day that Oldenburg became part of Metropolitan France) the military contingent of the duchy marched off to Osnabrück to enter French service as part of the 129th Line Infantry Regiment, which drew its conscripts from the '*Departements*' of the Weser estuary. (Some officers resigned their commissions rather than enter French service.) The 1st and 2nd Battalions of the 129th were brought up to full strength and then sent to Maastricht, where the 3rd Battalion was raised. The two complete battalions were then ordered to march for

Napoleon, Davout, Murat and others of his staff in Prussia
after his triumphant victories at Jena and Auerstädt in 1806.

Napoleon's entry into Berlin, 27 October 1806. Never had Prussia been so humiliated as on this day! A few short weeks after hot-blooded young Prussian officers had ostentatiously sharpened their swords on the steps of the French embassy, the Prussian army was shattered and almost annihilated and much of the country was under harsh French occupation. The dazed citizens of the capital had to watch as their hated conqueror rode in state through the Brandenburg Gate.

Russia and became part of the 10th Infantry Division of General Ledru in Marshal Ney's III Corps of the *Grande Armée*. The other units of the III Corps were:

10th Infantry Division
    24th Légère (French light infantry regiment)
      4 battalions
    26th French Line Infantry Regiment
    72nd French Line Infantry Regiment
      each of 3 or 4 battalions
    129th French Line Infantry Regiment
      2 battalions
    1st Portuguese Legion Infantry Regiment
      3 battalions
    One company of French foot artillery
    One company of French horse artillery

11th Infantry Division (General Razout)
    The Regiment Illyrien
    4th French Line Infantry Regiment
    12th French Line Infantry Regiment
    93rd French Line Infantry Regiment
      each of 4 or 5 battalions
    One company of foot and one company of horse artillery

25th Infantry Division (originally the Crown Prince of Württemberg, later General Marchand)
    1st & 2nd Württemberg Light Infantry Battalions
    1st & 2nd Württemberg Jäger (Rifle) Battalions
    1st, 2nd, 4th & 6th Württemberg Line Infantry Regiments (later also the 7th Württemberg Infantry Regiment)

Artillery Reserve
    Five foot artillery batteries

Total Artillery – 90 guns (including 30 Württemberg pieces in two horse and three foot batteries).

Light Cavalry Brigade (General Mouriez)
    4th French Chasseurs, 11th French Hussars, 4th Württemberg Jägers

Light Cavalry Brigade (General Beurmann)

    6th French Lancers, 1st & 2nd Württemberg Chevau-légers Regiments

In June 1812 the III Corps crossed the Russian border and advanced towards Moscow. Both battalions of the 129th took part in the Battle of Smolensk on 17 August 1812 but it is not recorded that they were presented with an eagle for their valour in this action, the first large battle of the campaign. For the next three months, until mid-November, the 129th remained in the Smolensk area on garrison duties, maintaining security along Napoleon's ever-extending and vulnerable lines of communication, which eventually reached into Moscow itself.

As the starving mob that was all that was left of the *Grand Armée* staggered back through Smolensk in the bitter winter of 1812, the 1st and 2nd Battalions of the 129th took part in the rear-guard action at Katowo on 18 November, an action which ended badly for the French. Ney's III Corps now formed the rearguard of Napoleon's army and it was ground to pieces by the relentless Russian troops in the bitter weather. Only a handful of officers and men of the 129th survived to reach their homeland again.

The 3rd Battalion of the 129th also contained Oldenburgers, and its history in this dramatic year is as follows. In May 1812 it marched to Berlin and then on through Magdeburg and Stettin to the Island of Rügen. In mid-November it advanced eastwards to Danzig and remained here until after Christmas. By mid-January 1813 the 3rd Battalion joined the remnants of the III Corps in Mulhausen, retiring with them on Küstrin and later to Spandau, where they became part of the garrison of this fortress. After Spandau capitulated in May 1813, the remnants of the 3rd Battalion marched back to their depot in Maastricht. As a result of a reorganisation of the French infantry the 129th was disbanded, the men being used to bring the 127th and 128th regiments up to strength.

The dispossessed Duke of Oldenburg had left his duchy in 1811 and had taken refuge in Russia where his second son was the Tsar Alexander's brother-in-law. Both his sons fought with distinction on the Russian side in the campaigns of 1812 and 1813. The duke himself was given the task by the Tsar of organising the 'Russian–German Legion'. This formation consisted of infantry, cavalry and artillery and was recruited from among German prisoners of war in Russian hands; on 29 March 1815 it was transferred into Prussian service, providing raw material for the 30th and 31st Infantry Regiments, the 8th Ulans, the 18th and 19th Horse Artillery Batteries and the 19th Artillery Park Column.

On 27 November 1813 Peter, Duke of Oldenburg, re-entered his duchy and set about re-raising his armed forces. These consisted of 800 line infantrymen and 800 Landwehr (Home Guard) organised in one regiment of two battalions each of four companies. There was a band of twenty-one musicians, and each company had three drummers. Commander of the regiment was Oberst (Colonel) Wardenburg, who had been a brigade commander in the Russian–German Legion.

The regiment was mobilised for the Hundred Days Campaign of 1815 and was attached to the North German Army of General Kleist von Nollendorf. This consisted of three infantry brigades, the Oldenburgers being part of the Anhalt–Thuringian Brigade of Major General von Egloffstein of Saxe–Weimar. This brigade contained a battalion each from Lippe–Detmold, Saxe–Weimar, Saxe–Gotha, Saxe–Anhalt, Waldeck and Schwarzburg; in all eight battalions with 6,800 men. A squadron of Hessian Dragoons was later attached to the brigade. The brigade was used to blockade the small French fortress of Bouillon and, later, to besiege Sedan and Mezieres.

The Battle History of Nassau's Troops

THE CAMPAIGNS OF 1806 AND 1807

Under the terms of the treaty governing the Confederation of the Rhine (Rheinbund), which Nassau joined on 12 July 1806, the military contingent which had to be provided for service with the French against Prussia, Saxony, Sweden, England and, later, Russia, was an infantry

Since 1961, no one rides in state through the Brandenburg Gate – the concrete wall in the foreground, built by the Communists, prevents all access.

brigade of four battalions and the *Jäger zu Pferde* (mounted rifles) regiment.

The infantry mobilised at the end of September 1806, and the 3rd (Jäger) Battalion was then ordered to Frankfurt am Main to join Marshal Augereau's III Corps. This corps took part in the battle of Jena on 14 October 1806, where the Prussian–Saxon army was decisively crushed by the French. The Nassau Jäger battalion marched thence with the III Corps to Berlin and then farther east to Driesen and Posen, following up the disorganised remnants of the once-proud Prussian army. They were then detached to escort a convoy of prisoners back to Magdeburg, where they met up again with their comrades of the 1st and 2nd Nassau Infantry Battalions who arrived there on 26 October 1806. The 4th Battalion remained in Hanau until 7 January 1807 and then marched for Berlin where it arrived on 15 February and was joined by the rest of the brigade, who were now used on convoy duties to Spandau, Magdeburg, Stettin and Warsaw. The Nassau *Jäger zu Pferde* regiment was now also mobilised at a strength of two companies, the 1st Company going to Berlin in May 1807. (On 15 October 1806 the Nassau troops were ordered to adopt the French system of rank badges to avoid confusion with their allies.)

The Nassauers were now attached to the VIII Corps of Marshal Mortier, who had the task of covering the northern flank of Napoleon's lines of communication. The main French army was operating far to the east against the allied Prussian

and Russian armies. Mortier's enemies in the north were the Swedes and their English Allies in Swedish Pomerania, which then included Stralsund and the island of Rügen.

After a Swedish raid had caused heavy losses to the French division of General Grandjean, the bulk of the Nassau infantry brigade was ordered to leave Berlin and to reinforce the now shaky French front. Oberst von Schäffer commanded the brigade and they reached Pasewalk on 15 April 1807, joining Marshal Mortier, who now commanded 12,000 men. Next day he attacked the Swedish force under General Armfeld at Ferdinandshoff, beat him soundly and pushed him back on Anklam. Mortier sent General Vaux with Oberst von Schäffer's Nassauers and the 72nd French Line Infantry Regiment to capture Uckermünde, which they did, taking 500 Swedes prisoner and capturing three guns at the same time. On 18 April Mortier entered into a ten-day armistice with the Swedes, and the Nassauers were transferred to reinforce the besieging force around Colberg, where the famous Prussian officer Leutnant Schill led a spirited defence, and in fact saved Prussia's honour in the dark years of 1806 and 1807. The Nassauers only stayed here for three days before being sent back to Berlin to rejoin the rest of their brigade.

On 26 June 1807, however, the 2nd, 3rd and 4th Nassau infantry battalions were back at Colberg which was still holding out, supplied with warlike materials by the Royal Navy. (Unfortunately, the British Board of Ordnance sent quantities of cannon barrels to Colberg, but no chassis to go with them; and as there was no suitable wood in the town to make these on the spot, the barrels just lay about until the siege was raised!) The Nassauers formed the 2nd Brigade of the besiegers, together with the 3rd French Light Infantry Regiment. The Treaty of Tilsit (9 July 1807) put an end to hostilities between France and Russia and Prussia.

Sweden was still in the ring against Napoleon, however, and England sent 8,000 men of the King's German Legion (see *The King's German Legion* in this series for details) to Rügen to support him. Napoleon therefore sent Marshal Brune with 40,000 men to end this insolence. Among Brune's troops was the Nassau brigade under Oberst von Schäffer which formed part of General Pino's Division. The Swedes, however, now found themselves alone when the English troops left them to take part in the attack on Copenhagen and the capture of the Danish fleet. The Swedish king, Gustav Adolf IV, withdrew into Stralsund and then across to the island of Rügen. Marshal Brune followed as quickly as possible but on 7 September 1807 peace was agreed upon and the French occupied Rügen unopposed. The Nassauers returned home, accompanied by several letters from their various commanders, praising their conduct in the past campaign.

THE 1809 CAMPAIGN AGAINST AUSTRIA

By this time the four infantry battalions had been reorganised into two regiments. The 2nd Regiment had marched off for Spain together with the 2nd Squadron of the *Jäger zu Pferde* regiment in September 1808, and the 1st Infantry Regiment was mobilised for the Austrian campaign and became part of General Dupas's Reserve Division of Marshal Davoust's Corps at Donauwörth on the river Danube. The division had the following units:

1st Regiment of Nassau (or 3rd Rheinbund-Regiment) – Oberst Pöllnitz
4th Rheinbund-Regiment (Saxon Duchies)
5th Rheinbund-Regiment (Anhalt and Lippe)
6th Rheinbund-Regiment (Schwarzburg, Reuss and Waldeck)

The Nassauers did not come into action during this campaign but were part of the garrison of Vienna from 22 June until 21 October 1809. During this time, Napoleon gave the regiment two cannon (taken from Vienna's arsenal) and ordered that a regimental artillery company should be formed. This step had already been taken by the French infantry of the Army of Germany before the battle of Wagram – a remarkable tactical 'gimmick' which had been generally abandoned in all European armies at the turn of the century. The Nassau regiment's artillerymen received their own uniform, with red plumes, epaulettes, collars and cuffs.

THE NASSAUERS IN THE PENSINSULAR WAR 1808–13

While the 1st Nassau Regiment was in Austria, the 2nd Regiment and one squadron of the Nassau 'Chasseurs à Cheval' were mobilised and sent to Spain to take part in what still stands as one of the most vicious and merciless campaigns in military history. There were refreshing occasions in these dark years when glimpses of chivalry lit up the bloody gloom but generally this war was conducted both by the Spanish and Portuguese on the one side and the French, Italians and Poles on the other (most German contingents retained their code of conduct and their discipline under the extremely adverse conditions in these cam-

Leib-Bataillon von Todenwarth, 1806 – a Knötel plate illustrating the uniform worn in the war of that year. The high black leather helmet with yellow metal furniture and stuffed black wool crest is similar, but not identical with that worn by the Bavarian cavalry of the day. The uniform is in the usual Nassau dark green but with red facings and yellow buttons and piping; the facings changed to black in 1809, and the helmets were also exchanged for brown fur colpacks of hussar pattern at that time. The white trousers and gaiters were summer wear; in winter grey breeches were worn inside black gaiters reaching to below the knee.

Frederick William, the 'Black Duke' of Brunswick. His father, a Prussian marshal, was killed in 1806 at Jena, and Frederick William swore to avenge him. His hostility to Napoleon caused him to be deposed in 1807; he fled to Austria where, in 1809, he raised the 'Black Horde' to fight the Corsican dictator. When Austria collapsed he fought his way to the North Sea coast and took his corps into British service until 1815; he was killed at Quatre-Bras.

An unusual early portrait of General Michel Ney, 1769–1815 – an oil painting by Brune now in the National Museum at Versailles. It shows Ney in hussar uniform, with his hair powdered and queued. He enlisted in 1787 in the cavalry which became the 5e *hussards*. His impetuosity at Jena imperilled his corps, but he distinguished himself in the pursuit which followed victory, taking 36,000 prisoners and 700 guns at Erfurt and Magdeburg. Arriving late on the field of Eylau, 8 February 1807, his command sealed the Russian defeat; and as commander of the French right at Friedland on 14 June 1807 he made a great contribution to the victory.

paigns) with mutual sadism and brutality. It must be mentioned that Napoleon's system of forcing his armies to live off the countries in which they were fighting was a major factor in generating, and maintaining, a high level of hostility among the Spanish and Portuguese populations against the occupation troops. Wellington's armies experienced no such problems even when in an enemy country (as in France in 1814) because they were regularly supplied by a highly developed logistic system which did not overstrain the economy of the country in which they were operating.

By November 1808 the 2nd Regiment of Nassau (with two battalions and commanded by Oberstleutnant (Lieutenant Colonel) von Kruse) and the 2nd Squadron of the Nassau Chasseurs à Cheval reached Burgos in northern Spain and became part of the IV Corps of General Sebastiani. The infantry regiment was in General Leval's 2nd Division:

1st Brigade Oberst von Porbeck (Baden) (killed at the battle of Talavera on 28 July 1809)
    2nd Nassau Infantry Regiment
        2 battalions
    4th Baden Infantry Regiment
        2 battalions
    One battery of Baden foot artillery
        6 guns
2nd Brigade General Chassé (Holland)
    Infantry Regiment 'Holland' (from 1810 the 123rd 'French' Line Infantry Regiment)
        2 battalions
    One company of Dutch sappers and miners
    One Dutch horse artillery battery
        6 guns

The Battle of Talavera, 28 July 1809 – the confusion of a Napoleonic battle is well conveyed by the artist of this scene, which from the proliferation of Spanish units seems to show the southern end of Wellington's line, near Talavera town on the river Tajo. It was at the junction of British and Spanish units that Leval's German Division was thrown by the French; contingents from Nassau, Baden, Berg, Westfalia and Hessen–Darmstadt suffered heavily. A little to the north, on Wellington's left, other Germans were fighting for the Allies – the Hanoverians of the King's German Legion. (*National Army Museum*)

3rd Brigade General Grandjean (France)
    Hessen–Darmstadt Infantry Regiment 'Gross und Erbprinz'
        2 battalions
    Infantry Regiment of Frenkfurt (Oberstleutnant von Welsch)
        1 battalion
    Parisian Guards
        1 battalion
Cavalry of the IV Corps
    3rd Dutch Hussars
        4 squadrons
    Westfalian Chevau-légers
        2 squadrons
    Nassau Chasseurs à Cheval
        1 squadron

The Nassauers were now armed and organised completely as for the French army (each battalion having one grenadier, four fusilier and one volti-geur company) and wore French badges of rank. Later in the campaign French drill regulations were also introduced. The 2nd Squadron of the Nassau Chasseurs à Cheval were commanded by a major and had also a Rittmeister (captain of cavalry), one first lieutenant and two second lieutenants, one surgeon, a quartermaster, a sergeant-major, a veterinary surgeon, a quarter-master's assistant, a rough-rider, eight sergeants, two trumpeters, eight corporals, and ninety-six troopers (Jägers) including a smith, a saddler and a waggon driver.

The Nassau units had an eventful time in Spain and casualties were very heavy, more men dying from disease than by enemy action. From 1809 until the end of 1811 the squadron of Chasseurs à Cheval received reinforcements from their depot totalling five officers, seven N.C.O.s and fifty-four troopers. In July 1813 the 1st Squadron joined their comrades in Spain and the 'Premier Régiment des Chasseurs de Nassau' as the French called them were used for security duties on the lines of communication of King Joseph's 'Army of the Centre'. They were skilful and daring horse-men whose bravery won them the respect of friend and foe alike; Bernays, in his *Schicksale des Grossherzogthums Frankfurt* devotes much time to

Nassau infantry uniforms, 1808–15 – a Knötel plate from the regimental history of the 1st Regiment, showing development over the seven-year period. On the *left* is an officer with bicorne, gorget, epaulettes, baldric and tasselled Hessian boots. His later counterpart of the French period (*background*) wears a French-style shako but retains all the other status items. *Second from left* and *third from left* are grenadiers, both with the usual French-style accoutrements of status – red plumes, epaulettes and sabre-knots – but both with special headgear. The first is a figure of 1808, with the Bavarian-style boiled-leather helmet with a black crest; the second is of 1810, with the hussar-type brown colpack with red bag and cords. The fusilier (*right*) has a shako plate bearing the regimental number 2. See colour plates and commentaries for further details.

their exploits, which are often of almost legendary proportions. Due to the hard campaigning and the poor forage in Spain, horse losses were high and it was not long before the Nassauers were mounted on the highly-blooded Andalusian horses.

By October 1813 the Nassau Chasseurs à Cheval were in action in Catalonia (north eastern Spain) and on 25 November of that year they, like all other German troops serving with the French armies, were disarmed and made prisoners of war. This was due to the recent events at the Battle of Leipzig when whole brigades of

Westfalians, Saxons and Württembergers had gone over to the Prussian–Russian–Austrian armies which were tightening their grasp around Napoleon's hard-pressed forces. The 1st Squadron was disarmed in Gerona, the 2nd in Fornells near Figueras. The strength of the regiment was then twelve officers and 231 men. The commander, Major Baron Oberkampf, wrote in a report to Marshal Suchet: 'During the last five years I have been in French service and I have received many flattering commendations of my conduct and of that of my regiment. I have obtained, and will retain, eternal proof of this in my receipt of the officers' cross of the Legion of Honour'. The men were interned in Perpignan and returned home in April 1814. Those still fit for military service were transferred to the reformed Nassau infantry regiments.

The 2nd Regiment of Nassau Infantry remained in the so-called German Division of General Leval and in October 1808 were part of Napoleon's force which marched via Vittoria, crossed the upper Ebro and reached Madrid via Burgos, Valladolid, the Duero, Segovia and L'Escorial.

In January 1809 the German Division left Madrid to block the bridges over the river Tajo (south of the city) to prevent the advance of a Spanish army. For this task the Division was augmented by the following French foreign units: 'Régiment Prusse', 'Régiment Westphalie' and the 'Légion Irlandais'. A number of minor clashes took place along the Tajo from Talavera to Almarez. Later the German division advanced south of the river and took part in the battles of Mesa de Ibor (17 March 1809) and Medellin on the river Guardiana (27 March 1809). In both these battles the 2nd Regiment of Nassau so distinguished itself that they wore these battle honours on their helmets until after the First World War. At Medellin the Spanish general Cuesta with 30,000 infantry, 7,000 cavalry and 30 guns was rash enough to attempt to stand up against Marshal Victor with 17,000 men. This may initially sound odd but, apart from two regiments of Swiss mercenaries, most of Cuesta's men were raw recruits, badly equipped peasants with little or no military training. Victor's men were by now all well-experienced, well-disciplined (in battle if not elsewhere!) and hard-bitten regulars. Cuesta was heavily defeated. Cuesta's force consisted of:

Infantry:
  4th Battalion, Spanish Guards
  2nd and 4th Battalion, Walloon Guards
  2nd Regiment of Majorca – 2 battalions
  2nd Battalion, Catalonian Light Infantry
  Provincial Battalion of Badajoz
  Provincial Grenadier Battalion
  Regiment Badajoz – 2 battalions
  Regiment Merida – 1 battalion
  Regiment La Serena – 1 battalion
  Regiment of Jaen – 2 battalions
  Regiment Irlanda – 2 battalions
  Provincials of Toledo – 1 battalion
  Provincials of Burgos – 1 battalion
  2nd Battalion, Voluntarios of Madrid
  3rd Battalion, Voluntarios of Seville
  Regiment of Campo Maior
  Provincials of Guadix
  Provincials of Cordova
  Regiment Osuna – 2 battalions
  Granaderos del General
  Tiradores de Cadiz

Total – about 20,000 bayonets

Cavalry
  1st Hussars of Estremadura (late 'María Luisa')
  4th Hussars (Voluntarios d'Espagne)
  Rey   ⎫ Regiments which had been sent to
           ⎪ Denmark in Marquis de La Romana's
  Infante ⎬ Division and had subsequently re-
           ⎪ turned on English ships to fight against
  Almanza ⎭ Napoleon
  Caçadores de Llerena ⎫
                    ⎬ new levies
  Imperial de Toledo ⎭
Most regiments had a squadron detached in Andalusia looking for remounts.

Total about 3,200 sabres

  Artillery – 30 guns and 650 men
  Sappers – two companies – 200 men

THE BATTLE OF TALAVERA
27–28 JULY 1809

In his first attempt to operate against the French in Spain, the Marquis Wellesley (later Duke of Wellington) moved out from his base in Portugal and advanced against Madrid in conjunction

Officer of the Nassau Reitende Jäger, 1806–8; a plate by Weiland from his work *Darstellung der Kaiserlich Franzosischen Armee* 1812, in which the French and their allies are portrayed. Weiland sub-titles this plate 'Nassau Usingschen Cheveux Leger Officier', and the figure obviously served as one of Knötel's sources for his plate of four of the men of this regiment. Knötel mistook the sabretasche cypher – clearly FA – and also omitted the bandolier picker equipment. The helmet shown here is definitely of Bavarian cavalry pattern but the green plume rising from the front of the crest remains a mystery. (See colour plates.)

with a Spanish army under the same General Cuesta. Strengths were: English, Portuguese and Germans – 20,000; Spanish – 32,000. Most of the Spanish forces had been involved in the débâcle of Medellin and thus their morale was, at the best, brittle. With this in mind, Wellesley put the Spanish troops in, and to the north of, the town of Talavera on the river Tajo; the English, Portuguese and German troops (King's German Legion) were extended north of the Spaniards to the hills about two miles away, and were arranged behind the Arrojo Morapejo stream.

2nd Nassau Infantry Regiment in Spain, 1810. By this time both regiments were organised on the French model, each battalion consisting of one grenadier, one light or voltigeur, and four fusilier companies. Knötel shows a soldier of each type of company. The voltigeur (*left*) wears a shako with a bugle-horn badge surrounding the regimental number, green pompon, green epaulettes with yellow crescents, green sabre-knot, and yellow cords and yellow-tipped green plume. The grenadier (*centre*) wears red epaulettes and sabre-knot, and red bag, cords, pompon, and plume, attached to a brown fur colpack. The fusilier (*right*) wears a tufted company-colour pompon on his shako and a yellow plate with regimental number. His shoulder-straps are green piped yellow. Note that unlike French centre-company men, who had abandoned the side-arm, he wears a sabre – the knot would have been plain yellow-buff leather.

King Joseph, with his 46,000 strong Army of the Centre, moved against Wellesley from Madrid and attacked the Allies on the night of 27 July; the battle was violent but the Allies held even though the Spanish army was paralysed and ineffective from the start of the action. The assault was renewed next day with the German division once again in the forefront of the combat just north of Talavera. But all the French and German valour in these attacks was in vain; Wellesley's line held fast and after the battle King Joseph had to fall back on Madrid. The losses of the German Division were 103 dead, 827 wounded and 77

captured; as their total strength in the battle was 4,267 men this meant 25 per cent losses.

The 1st Regiment of Nassau was sent to join the VII Corps under Marshal Augereau in Catalonia (north east Spain) and attached to General Rouyer's Division at Barcelona, which in March 1810 consisted of:

1st Brigade (General Schwarz – French)
  1st Regiment of Nassau
    2 battalions   1,494 men
  4th Rheinbund Regiment (Saxon Duchies)
    3 battalions   929 men
2nd Brigade (Colonel Chambaud – Saxony–Anhalt)
  5th Rheinbund Regiment
    2 battalions   1,258 men
  6th Rheinbund Regiment
    2 battalions   876 men

The Spanish forces in Catalonia under General O'Donnell were conducting guerrilla operations with the aim of breaking the communications between the French III and VII Corps and then of destroying their hated enemies in detail. As usual, the Spanish forces of this era were no match for the French and their allies in the open field, but concentrated on cutting off isolated detachments and destroying them in ambushes.

Augereau gave them one such opportunity when on 19 March 1810 he sent General Schwarz's brigade to the remote Spanish-held town of Manresa (then a flourishing gunpowder manufacturing centre for the Spaniards) with orders to occupy the town and to destroy the powder-mills but with no instructions as to when to return to their base at Barcelona. (This is probably the first military application of the 'use and throw away' principle!) Leaving Barcelona on 19 March, Schwarz's brigade stormed the pass of Mont Serrat and on 21st reached the target – Manresa. The town was deserted except for the old and sick, and the brigade entered and put it into a state of defence, for already the surrounding hills were filling up with thousands of Spanish armed peasants who finally outnumbered the brigade by six to one. Manresa was now in a state of siege and only parties of over company strength could venture out of the town.

On the 25 March an ammunition convoy escorted by a battalion of the French 67th Line Infantry Regiment arrived in Manresa, having lost two of its waggons *en route* from Barcelona and having been saved from massacre only by the timely arrival of the 2nd Battalion and both élite (flank) companies of the 1st Battalion of the Nassau Regiment, who had come out of Manresa to meet them. The French battalion left again on 27 March to fight its way back to Barcelona, and on 2 April was given the unenviable task of escorting a second convoy of ammunition to the beleaguered force in Manresa. General O'Donnell and his Spaniards captured this convoy and the few survivors of the escort who staggered back to Barcelona convinced Marshal Augereau that General Schwarz's brigade was lost. In fact, the situation in Manresa was so desperate that Schwarz at last decided to abandon the town during the night of the 4/5 April; his food was exhausted, ammunition and powder very low, and only by stripping the church roof and melting down pewter plate could he provide his surviving men with even 30 rounds each. The wounded had to be abandoned in the care of some Spanish monks even though this usually meant a slow death for the poor wretches at the hands of the Spanish women. Miraculously, Manresa proved an exception to the rule; the Spanish monks defended their charges from the peasants with force of arms when they streamed back into the abandoned town, and the wounded were handed over to the Spanish army.

Schwarz's attempt to slip through the enemy lines unnoticed failed when at about midnight the Spanish sentries heard them and gave the alarm. At once the church bells in all near-by villages began ringing – a signal for the militia to turn out – and the chase to Barcelona was on. In the darkness the column of Schwarz's brigade became separated and the 2nd Battalion of the 1st Regiment of Nassau struck off on the wrong path, only picking up the correct one again after finding fresh horse dung on one of the roads leading from a junction, which indicated that mounted officers had shortly before ridden that way. Under continuous fire from all sides the column joined up again at daybreak and pushed on as fast as possible towards Barcelona and safety. Many men dropped out from exhaustion on the way and once the brigade had to stop and fight a rear-guard action to ease the pursuit and to allow the men a little rest in the blazing sun. All day the chase con-

The Oldenburg Rheinbund contingent in 1810 – a Knötel plate. Shortly before being absorbed into Metropolitan France, Oldenburg raised an infantry regiment which was dressed in the singular uniform illustrated here. The coat is very Prussian: dark blue, double-breasted, and with red facings. The hat worn by the fusiliers and light company is, however, reminiscent of the headgear worn by Austrian Jägers, artillery, pontoniers and engineers at this time. The officers wore the braid straps for epaulette attachment on their shoulders, but not, apparently, epaulettes – perhaps these were reserved for parade and gala dress. The grenadiers wore French-type bearskins.

tinued, but by evening the pursuit slackened and the brigade bivouacked at St Andres, having been marching and fighting for over twenty hours. Next day, 6 April, to the great astonishment of the garrison of Barcelona who had given them up for dead, Schwarz's brigade marched into the city with bands playing. Augereau had already ordered the quartermaster of the Nassau Regiment to take stock of all his stores and hand them in as his regiment had been captured! The Nassauers' losses were high:

	Officers	N.C.O.s	Men
Dead	3	6	33
Wounded	10	25	168
Captured	5	12	58
Missing	—	18	146
TOTALS	18	61	405

The gates of Spandau fortress; to the north-west of Berlin, it had been one of the city's strongest defences for centuries. Although in good repair in 1806 it was shamefully surrendered to the French after the collapse of the Prussian army. The Nassauers were here later in that campaign. Under French command in 1813, Spandau held out stubbornly against Russian and Prussian besiegers. Today the citadel houses a small museum and the bastions, still in good repair, can be visited.

The Ducal Saxon regiment had lost 353 officers and men. Augereau published the following order of the day to praise the considerable achievements of these German troops in his Corps:

Barcelona 6 April 1810

His Excellency Marshal of the Empire, commander in chief of the Army of Catalonia, charges General de Division Rouyer to relay to General Schwartz and to the superior officers of his German Brigade detached to Manresa his complete satisfaction for the brilliant conduct of their troops particularly in the series of various combats which they fought against superior forces.

General Schwartz responded perfectly to the intentions of the mission with which His Excellency charged him. That general officer is to commend to His Excellency those of his officers and soldiers who have particularly distinguished themselves.

Augereau

When one considers that the Manresa expedition was a very representative example of the sort of life that French units in Spain endured from 1809–13 it is easy to see how the 'running sore' of this campaign drained the resources of trained manpower and warlike materials of the French Empire.

So life for the 1st Regiment of Nassau went on – grinding, boring garrison duty being relieved by periods of intense and exhausting activity as task forces were sent out into the hostile hills to attempt to bring the elusive foe to battle.

On 10 July 1811 Oberst von Pöllnitz, commander of the 1st Nassau Regiment was killed by a cannon shot from a British ship at Mataro near Tarragona, and his place was taken by Oberstleutnant von Steuben until 28 February 1812 when Oberst Meder was transferred from the 2nd Nassau Regiment and promoted to fill the post.

In August 1812 the garrison of Barcelona (1st Regiment of Nassau, 18th French Light, 5th and 115th French Line Infantry Regiments, some cavalry detachments and the artillery – 10,000 men in all) was issued with bread (itself a rarity!) which had been poisoned by the Spanish workers who had brought in the flour. Luckily there were no fatal casualties as a result of this but on other occasions this, and other French garrisons in Spain lost numbers of men due to poisoning.

Reinforcements for the Nassauers came to Barcelona in July 1812 (4 officers, 24 N.C.O.s and 426 men) and in June 1813 (20 N.C.O.s and 238 men).

Napoleon's disastrous defeat in Russia in 1812 turned the tide of war against him in Spain as well, and the French were gradually pushed up out of the peninsula and into France. In June 1813 the British General Murray landed in Catalonia with an international force of 20,000 men and besieged Tarragona. General Mathieu was sent from Barcelona with the entire garrison of the city (6,000 men) to relieve Tarragona but

Murray had by then already re-shipped his army (losing most of his heavy equipment in his haste), and Mathieu returned to Barcelona. Murray was sacked for his timidity; General Lord Bentinck took his place and re-invested Tarragona, so the Barcelona garrison once again came to its aid. Marshal Suchet (now commanding in Catalonia) decided to destroy the fortress of Tarragona and to abandon it, which he did on 18 August 1813.

As already mentioned, Napoleon's German allies began abandoning him at about this time and Nassau officially joined his enemies on the 16 November 1813. In accord with secret orders, the 2nd Regiment of Nassau went over to the English on 10 December. No such secret orders reached the unlucky 1st Regiment (vast amounts of French despatches were captured by the Spanish guerrillas in this war) and although Lord Clinton, commander of the English forces in Catalonia, sent Oberst Meder a letter from Oberst Kruse urging him, Meder, to follow his example and to bring his troops over to the English, Meder proudly refused (as he thought) to sully his military honour. On 22 December 1813 the 1st Regiment of Nassau was disarmed in Barcelona and escorted to French prisons by the 117th French Line Infantry Regiment. The authorities did not trust the 5th, 115th French Line or the 18th French Light Infantry Regiments to do this job as these regiments had shared the fortunes of their Nassau comrades and it was feared that they would have allowed their prisoners to escape. Oberst Meder seems to have done well for himself; after the disarming of his regiment he entered French service. Fate caught up with him a few weeks later, however, when he was killed just outside Barcelona fighting the Spanish.

THE WATERLOO CAMPAIGN

On 9 May 1815 Nassau concentrated her forces (two infantry regiments each of two line and one Landwehr battalions, each of one Grenadier, four Jäger (three in the Landwehr battalion) and one Flanquer company. Commander of the 1st Regiment was Oberst von Steuben; Oberst von Kruse was promoted General and commanded the Nassau contingent.

The 1st Regiment was part of the Hanoverian Reserve Corps under Lieutenant General von der Decken which was organised as follows:

1st Brigade (Lieutenant-Colonel von der Decken)
  Feld-Bataillon Hoya
  Landwehr-Bataillon Mölln
  Landwehr-Bataillon Bremerlehe
2nd Brigade (Lieutenant-Colonel von Beaulieu)
  Landwehr-Bataillon Nordheim
  Landwehr-Bataillon Ahlefeldt
  Landwehr-Bataillon Springe
3rd Brigade (Lieutenant-Colonel Bodecker)
  Landwehr-Bataillon Otterndorf
  Landwehr-Bataillon Celle
  Landwehr-Bataillon Ratzeburg

'The Happy Hunter' – a cartoonist's view of Napoleon after the Battle of Leipzig in 1813. The text of the verse, very loosely translated and with no attempt at rhyming, reads: 'He always stays calm and unruffled; He's not the best or worst because he has shot (?); If his expression is not too happy, It's because he smells the goat's tail.'

4th Brigade (Lieutenant-Colonel Wissel)
    Landwehr-Bataillon Hannover
    Landwehr-Bataillon Uelzen
    Landwehr-Bataillon Neustadt
    Landwehr-Bataillon Diepholz
                        Hannoverian total – 9,000 men
Nassau Contingent (General von Kruse)
    1st Nassau Infantry Regiment   –   2,880 men

The 2nd Regiment of Nassau was detached and placed together with the Regiment of Oranien–Nassau (Nassauers in Dutch–Belgian service) in the 2nd Dutch–Belgian Division of Leutnant General Baron de Perponcher in the Prince of Orange's I Corps:

1st Brigade (Major-General Baron de Bylandt)
    7th Line Infantry Regiment
       701 men
    27th Jäger Battalion
       809 men
    5th Militia Battalion
       482 men
    7th Militia Battalion
       675 men
    8th Militia Battalion
       566 men
2nd Brigade (H.R.H. Prince Bernhard of Saxe–Weimar)
    2nd Regiment of Nassau (3 battalions)
       2,709 men
    Regiment of Oranien–Nassau (2 battalions)
       1,591 men
Artillery (Major van Opstal)
    Horse battery – Captain Byleveld
    Foot battery – Captain Stievenaar
    This division was present at the battle of Quatre-Bras.

It would be beyond the scope of this book to describe the entire battle of Waterloo in detail. We must concentrate on the participation of the Nassauers themselves.

On 15 June 1815 the vital cross-roads of Quatre-Bras – lying between the Allied British and Prussian armies – was held only by the 2nd Nassau and the Nassau–Oranien Infantry Regiments and the attached battery of eight Dutch Horse Artillery guns.

THE NASSAUERS AT QUATRE-BRAS

The left wing of Wellington's army on the eve of Quatre-Bras was the 2nd Division of General Perponcher, in the area of Genappe, Frasnes and Nivelles. The 2nd Nassau Regiment was around Quatre-Bras (the 2nd Battalion being south of this place with a battery of Netherlands horse artillery, was the unit closest to the expected French advance from the south). At the appearance of the enemy, the division was to concentrate on the vital cross-roads at Quatre-Bras.

On the 15th Napoleon sent Marshal Ney ('The Bravest of the Brave') north towards Brussels with instructions to take Quatre-Bras and thus to prevent a unification of Wellington's army with that of Blücher (troops of Prussia and other German states). Ney's force consisted of the I Corps (General d'Erlon), the II Corps (General Reille), General Piré's Light Cavalry Division and (initially) the Chasseurs and Lanciers of the Imperial Guard.

Although the 2nd Division at Quatre-Bras had heard heavy cannon fire from the Prussian positions at Ligny early on the 15th, no great alarm was caused because it was interpreted as just another Prussian artillery practice and at that time no communication existed between the two Allied armies. In fact, this cannonade was audible expression of the desperate fight then taking place as Napoleon's simple, but terribly effective plan of destroying his separated enemy in detail before they could unite was put into practice. When, by the afternoon, the firing had not died down, Major von Normann, with the 2nd Battalion of the 2nd Regiment, and the Netherlands horse artillery battery, took up battle stations behind the village of Frasnes with patrols south towards Gosselies and informed the regimental commander of his actions. This intelligence was in turn relayed to headquarters, 2nd Division.

At about 6 pm Piré's advance guard drove in Normann's patrols and soon Normann was forced to fall back on Quatre-Bras, his pre-determined

Map of Quatre-Bras, showing position of Nassau and Nassau–Oranien ('Orange–Nassau') contingents. Key to place names: (1) Gemioncourt Farm, (2) Lairalle Farm, (3) Grand Pierrepont Farm, (4) Petit Pierrepont Farm, (5) Marais (6) Frasnes les Rous.

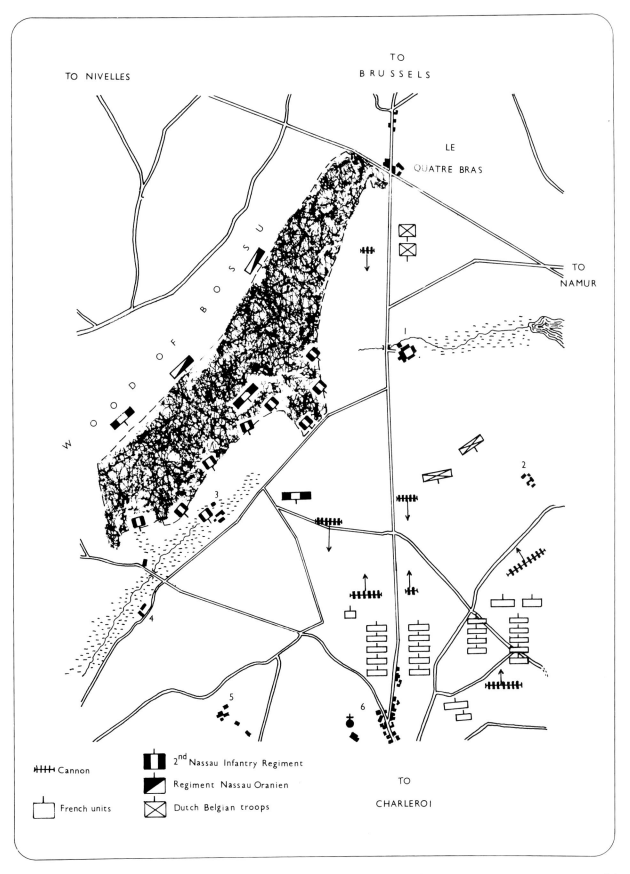

TO NIVELLES

TO
BRUSSELS

LE
QUATRE BRAS

TO
NAMUR

W O O D   O F   B O S S U

1

2

3

4

5

6

TO

CHARLEROI

╫╫╫ Cannon

French units

2ⁿᵈ Nassau Infantry Regiment

Regiment Nassau Oranien

Dutch Belgian troops

21

Interesting engraving by J. Voltz showing French prisoners being transported through a Bavarian town in 1814. The motley collection appears to include infantry, carabiniers, cuirassiers, hussars and chasseurs. The mounted escort visible with drawn sabre behind the cart seems to be a trooper of the 7th National Chevau-légers Regiment of Bavaria, talking to a Bavarian hussar trooper.

rallying point where the 2nd Brigade of the 2nd Division was also in position. Nightfall ended the fighting.

(The dispositions of the Nassauers at Quatre-Bras on 16 June may be seen on the map on page 21). At 6 am on 16 June the Prince of Orange (who had arrived there during the night and assumed command) ordered von Normann's battalion to push south to Frasnes and reconnoitre. Normann chased off light French cavalry picquets and reoccupied his position of the previous day. At 11 am the Duke of Wellington arrived and ordered von Normann to engage the enemy with two companies. Combat followed but remained at low-intensity. By now there were 7,000 men, 16 guns and 50 Prussian hussars under the Prince of Orange at Quatre-Bras; Wellington instructed him to hold his position until help arrived and then rode off to confer with Blücher over a common operational plan for the coming battle.

At 2 pm Ney, with 9,000 infantry, 1,850 cavalry and 22 guns began a very cautious assault on the Quatre-Bras position (Normann's force had by now withdrawn into the main Netherlands line). Despite tough resistance, the French soon occupied Piroaumont and Gemioncourt, the Allies being much hampered by their almost total lack of cavalry (the 50 Prussian hussars had also returned to their parent corps

during the day). The position was beginning to look grim for Perponcher's division when at last reinforcements came up. They were General von Merlen's Netherlands Brigade and General Picton's English division (altogether 7,000 infantry, 1,100 cavalry and 12 guns). Shortly after this the Duke of Brunswick ('The Black Duke') also arrived with part of his division (3,000 infantry and 800 cavalry) and the balance of power tipped slightly in favour of the Allies.

Encouraged by these new forces, the rash and impulsive Prince of Orange launched a hurried attack to win back most of the plateau which he had lost but was repulsed with losses. Wellington then returned from his meeting with Blücher and assumed command. Ney launched an assault to follow up his withdrawing enemy and Wellington countered – the struggle raged back and forth for some time – the young and untried Brunswick hussars being overthrown by the French Chasseurs à Cheval of Piré's command and the frenzied energies of the Prince of Orange contributing as much to the enemy's success as to that of his own troops. By the early evening, with reinforcements on both sides, the Allies had 37,000 men against Ney's 21,000 on the battlefield. At 7 pm Ney broke off his assaults and withdrew south to Frasnes. The day had cost about 4,000 dead and wounded on each side. The Allies bivouacked on the battlefield, the Prince of Orange resumed his position on Wellington's staff and gave up command of his brigade. The 1st Regiment of

Map of Waterloo, showing positions of Nassau and Nassau–Oranien contingents. Symbols representing units do not relate to actual size of unit or tactical formation. Key to place names: (1) Mont St Jean Farm, (2) Hougoumont, (3) La Haye Sainte, (4) Papelotte, (5) Smohain, (6) La Belle Alliance, (7) Plancenoit, (8) Rossome. At Waterloo the detailed deployment of the contingents was as follows:
Hougoumont Garrison (*General Byng*): 1st Bn., 2nd Regt. of Nassau (Hauptmann Büsgen) – companies shown individually on map. Two companies of Hannoverians. Four companies of British Foot Guards. Leib-Bataillon, Avantgarde, and 1st Light Bn. of Brunswick Corps.
The Centre: Front rank – 1st Bn., 1st Regt. of Nassau. Rear rank – 2nd Bn., 1st Regt. of Nassau. La Haye Sainte Garrison (Major Bäring, KGL) – both Flanquer companies, 1st Regt. of Nassau, together with 2nd Light Bn. KGL, Hannoverian Landwehr-Bn. Lüneburg, and light troops of other KGL battalions.
The Left Flank: From west to east: 2nd Bn., 2nd Regt. of Nassau; Landwehr-Bn., 2nd Regt. of Nassau; 1st Bn., Regiment Nassau–Oranien; 2nd Bn., Regiment Nassau–Oranien; Freiwillige Jäger Coy., Regiment Nassau–Oranien; *Papelotte* (*Hauptmann von Rettberg*) Flanquer coy., 3rd Bn., 2nd Regt. of Nassau, shown by platoons on map.

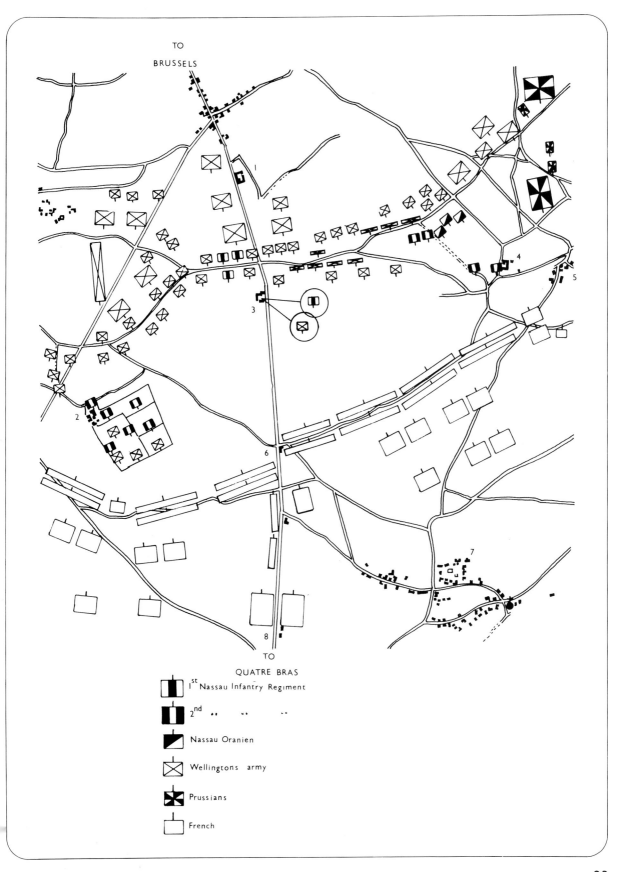

TO
BRUSSELS

TO
QUATRE BRAS

1ˢᵗ Nassau Infantry Regiment

2ⁿᵈ „ „ „ „

Nassau Oranien

Wellingtons army

Prussians

French

23

Nassau's flags, like those of most European armies of the day, were nailed to the staffs. The presentation of colours to a regiment was a great occasion, and the king or his representative – in the case of Prussia, the scene of the ceremony illustrated here – would be on hand to strike in the first of the gold-headed nails with a suitably decorative hammer. Lesser dignitaries would then each strike in one of the other nails. Holes were bored in the staff beforehand to prevent possible embarrassment!

Nassau arrived at Quatre-Bras only in the evening and did not take part in the day's fighting. That same day, 16 June, Blücher's army had been beaten by Napoleon at Ligny and was now withdrawing north-east on Wavre, but Wellington did not receive news of this until the morning of the 17th.

The 18 June 1815

Having successfully disengaged from Ney at Quatre-Bras, Wellington now concentrated his British–German–Dutch–Belgian army at Mont St Jean.

The 1st Regiment of Nassau was in the centre of the position, which was composed also of General Cooke's British Guards Division and General Alten's British Division and was commanded by the Prince of Orange – whose impetuous and overbearing decisions had cost many Allied lives at Quatre-Bras and were to cause the destruction of the 5th Line Battalion of the King's German Legion this day. From west to east the dispositions of the centre were as follows:

North of Hougoumont up against the road to Nivelles was Byng's British Guards Brigade of two battalions, then Maitland's Guards Brigade also two battalions, General Colin Halkett's British Brigade with four battalions, General Kielmannsegge's Hannoverian Brigade of five bat-

talions, and finally the King's German Legion Brigade of Colonel Ompteda with four battalions.

The left flank of Ompteda's brigade reached to the Genappe road and the farm of La Haye Sainte (in front of this brigade) was occupied by the 2nd Light Battalion of the King's German Legion. The 1st Regiment of Nassau was in the second line behind the brigades of Halkett and Kielmannsegge.

The brigades were arranged in two lines; the battalions in column. In the 1st Nassau Regiment the first line consisted of the 1st Battalion in divisional columns; the second line was formed by the 2nd and the Landwehr Battalions, both in assault columns. The 2nd Regiment of Nassau was on the western and eastern ends of Wellington's line, north of Hougoumont (where the 1st Battalion of this regiment took part in the defence of this vital farm, the struggle for which absorbed so much of Napoleon's generals' interest and energy (in vain) throughout the whole battle) and north of Papelotte – see below. In spite of being in the second of Wellington's battle lines and being situated on the reverse slope of the position, the 1st Regiment of Nassau suffered heavily in the artillery bombardment which began at 11 o'clock and went on all day – most of the shots which struck the regiment being ricochets.

By 2 pm a heavy French infantry assault (D'Erlon's Corps and Durutte's division) was in progress against Wellington's centre and left and a fierce struggle was centred around the farm of La Haye Sainte. In addition to the original garrison of this place (2nd Light Battalion, King's German Legion) two companies of the 1st Light Battalion, King's German Legion and 200 men (both Flanquer companies) of the line battalions of the 1st Regiment of Nassau were called in to reinforce this important post. By 3 pm this French assault had failed, and a massive cavalry attack began to develop against Wellington's centre and right flanks. This glittering mass of horsemen charged through the intervals between the battalions in the first of Wellington's lines (who had already formed square to receive them) and then descended upon the 1st Nassau Regiment which was also in square. As the vast majority of the Nassauers were young recruits in their first action, their conduct in this crisis was difficult to forecast

1 **Private, 1st Battalion, summer dress, 1803**

2 **Drummer, 2nd Battalion, summer campaign dress, 1806**

3 **Fusiliers, 4th Battalion, summer campaign dress, 1806**

1 **Fusilier, 2nd Battalion, parade dress, 1806**

2 **Grenadier sergeant, 4th Battalion, winter parade dress, 1806**

3 **Rifleman, 3rd Battalion, summer parade dress, 1806**

Nassau: Officers, Reitende Jäger, parade dress, 1807

1 Pioneer, 1st Infantry Regiment, 1809–13

2 Officer, Reitende Jäger, 1810 (in Spain)

3 Trooper, Reitende Jäger, parade dress, 1806

1 Officer (Premierleutnant) of Voltigeurs,
parade dress, 1810

2 Voltigeur Corporal, campaign dress, 1809–13

3 Drummer of Fusiliers, 2nd Infantry
Regiment, 1809–13

E

1 Oldenburg: Corporal, Voltigeur Company, 1808–11

2 Nassau: Sergeant-major of Grenadiers, 1st Regiment, 1815

3 Oldenburg: Drummer, Grenadier Company, drill order

1

3

2

1 Fusilier sergeant, 129th 'French' Line
  Infantry Regiment, 1812

2 Officer, Regiment Oldenburg, winter parade
  dress, 1814

3 Private, Freiwillige Jäger Detachment of the
  Regiment Oldenburg, field dress, 1814

1 Jäger, 1st Infantry Regiment, 1815
  (at Waterloo)

2 Officer of the General Staff, parade dress,
  1815

3 Officer of Grenadiers, 1st Infantry Regiment,
  1815

and, if they wavered, it could have caused Wellington's centre to break. Buoyed up by the excellent example of their British Allies in Halkett's brigade, who had held their fire until the cavalry was at a range of 60 paces and had then mown down dozens of horses and riders, the young Nassauers stood firm and repulsed the French cuirassiers' attacks. English dragoons then counterattacked the dismayed French cavalry and pushed them down the slope towards their own lines. This brought no relief to the long-suffering infantry, however; as soon as the cavalry had gone, the great battery of French artillery opened up on the English lines again and casualties began to mount.

A second massive cavalry attack followed at about 5 pm and the much weakened Allied squares in Wellington's centre almost vanished beneath the flood of sabres and helmets. But even now, in this moment of crisis when Wellington's slim reserves were committed, Bülow's Prussian corps began to appear from the east through the villages of Conture and Hanotelet, and gradually a flanking pressure was brought to bear on Napoleon's line. In spite of this, it was well over an hour before the French cavalry fell back from the Allied centre in this second attack, and over ten separate charges were made; but no squares broke.

At 6 pm the situation of the small garrison in the farm of La Haye Sainte became untenable when their ammunition supplies ran out. Major Bäring (of the King's German Legion) who commanded this outpost had repeatedly sent messages to the rear asking for ammunition resupply but for some reason none arrived. Now the French attackers could shoot down the defenders with impunity and Major Bäring was forced to withdraw up the hill to the main British line. The French swarmed after him and a battery of guns was set up about 300 paces in front of the 1st Battalion of the 1st Nassau Regiment and began to tear this and other units to shreds with discharges of canister. In a few minutes all officers of the Nassau grenadier company were dead or wounded. In an effort to put an end to the slaughter, the 1st Battalion's commander, Major von Weyhers, ordered a bayonet charge to take the battery but a few seconds later he was badly wounded by canister and the charge came to a halt. Wellington then sent an order that the battalion should return to its place in the line but for some reason the grenadier and the 1st Jäger company remained halted in a fire-fight with the French battery. Suddenly some French cuirassier squadrons, who had regathered by the guns, swarmed over the isolated Nassauers and cut them down. Between 7 and 8 pm Napoleon, seeing the growing power of the Prussians in his right rear and being as yet unable to break the Allied army on his front, decided to chance everything on one last desperate throw. The Imperial Guard, invincible in battle (largely because it had so rarely been used!) was launched at Wellington's army with the aim of bursting through his tired and weakened line and thus opening the way to Brussels. The incredible happened: the Imperial Guard was met by the steady British line and thrown back with heavy loss! The entire French army groaned in despair; the day was lost, and the French began to stream away to the south, fleeing in increasing confusion from the Prussians who had taken over the pursuit. On Wellington's left flank the assault columns of the Middle Guard were met by Halkett's brigade and the 1st Regiment of Nassau (now commanded by the Crown Prince of the Netherlands); General von Kruse and Oberst von Steuben were also there. The prince was wounded but the Guard was also pushed back. Napoleon's last effort had been made and had failed; the Battle of Waterloo had been won by the Anglo–Dutch–German Allies and the feared and hated dictator of Europe had his claws drawn for the last time.

The 2nd Regiment of Nassau at Waterloo

At 10 am the 1st Battalion, 2nd Regiment of Nassau, had been sent into the farm of Hougoumont on Wellington's right flank together with some Brunswickers, two Hannoverian companies, four companies of British Guards and General Cooke's British division. The 2nd and 3rd Battalions of the 2nd Regiment of Nassau and the Regiment of Orange–Nassau were on the extreme left flank of Wellington's line, and the village of Papelotte was occupied by the Flanquer company (under Hauptmann von Rettberg) of the 3rd Battalion, 2nd Regiment of Nassau. The map on

General Kleist von Nollendorf, commander of the North German Army Corps in the Hundred Days campaign. The Oldenburg Regiment was part of this corps. Kleist's uniform is dark blue with red facings and gold buttons, embroidery and shoulder cords. Among his decorations can be seen the Iron Cross (created in 1813 by King Frederick William III of Prussia), the Prussian Order of the Black Eagle, the Austrian Maria-Theresia Order, and the Russian Star of the Order of St George.

page 23 shows the dispositions of the Nassauers this fateful day. Just before 4 pm a heavy French assault on Papelotte forced Hauptmann von Rettberg to abandon the outlying village houses and to withdraw his company into the main building in the hamlet. Now the 10th, 11th and 12th Companies of his regiment came to his aid and the French were expelled again. The 2nd Regiment of Nassau remained in possession of Papelotte until the end of the battle. From about 4 pm onwards, von Bülow's 30,000 strong Prussian corps began deploying into combat formation on the eastern edge of the battlefield and advanced towards the French right rear at La Belle Alliance. They were opposed by Lobau's French corps and a fierce fight developed in the burning village of Plancenoit from which the French were ultimately driven. Hauptmann von Rettberg, with the four companies of the 2nd Regiment of Nassau under his command, joined in the Prussian assault on Plancenoit.

Most accounts of the Battle of Waterloo are remarkably vague as to the correct state of affairs in Papelotte and as to the actual participation in the battle of the 2nd Regiment of Nassau.

As its part of the booty taken after Waterloo, Nassau received four 6-pounder cannon, two 7-pounder howitzers and 12 train vehicles. As part of the reorganisation of the German mini-states which took place in 1815, Nassau had lost some land to Prussia and all inhabitants of this lost territory became Prussians. Thus, on 28 November 1815, 832 men of the 2nd Regiment were transferred to Prussian service and were replaced by 832 men of the Regiment of Orange–Nassau.

The Regiment of Orange–Nassau was disbanded on 3 January 1816, the men going into the 1st Nassau Infantry Regiment or to Prussia according to their place of birth. The Landwehr Battalion of the 1st Regiment of Nassau was also disbanded, those N.C.O.s and officers who were transferred to it to help in the training returned to their parent unit.

Until 1820 the 2nd Regiment of Nassau (at a strength of three battalions) served with the Netherlands army and was then reduced to two battalions on returning home.

The two Nassau infantry regiments were absorbed into the Prussian army in 1860 and assumed the titles:

Das 1te Herzogliche Nassauische Infanterie-Regiment Nr 87

and

Das 2te Herzogliche Nassauische Infanterie-Regiment Nr 88

The 2nd Regiment wore on its helmets the battle honours 'La Belle Alliance', 'Medellin' and 'Mesa de Ibor' until after the First World War.

The 1st Regiment wore 'La Belle Alliance'.

NASSAU ORDER OF BATTLE 1815

1st Infantry Regiment – Oberst von Steuben (71 officers and 2,974 men)

1st Battalion	–	Major von Weyhers
2nd Battalion	–	Major von Nauendorf
Landwehr Battalion	–	Major von Preen

2nd Infantry Regiment – Oberst Prinz Bernhard von Sachsen-Weimar (later Major Sattler) (89 officers, 2,738 men)

1st Battalion	–	Hauptmann Büsgen
2nd Battalion	–	Major Ph. von Normann
Landwehr Battalion	–	Major Hegmann

This regiment, together with the Regiment of Orange–Nassau, formed the 2nd Brigade of Lieutenant General Perponcher's 2nd Division of the Netherlands Army.

The Regiment of Orange Nassau (Nassau–Oranien) This

regiment was in Dutch–Belgian service and was part of the Netherlands Army.

1st Battalion
2nd Battalion } 39 officers, 1,427 men

Freiwillige Jäger Company – 3 officers, 166 men

Total Nassau troops – 193 officers and 6,832 men

[From a letter by General von Kruse to the Hanoverian Captain Beme]

Wiesbaden 7 January 1836

'. . . The Ducal Nassau Brigade, consisting of two infantry regiments was dispersed from 15–18 June 1815. The 2nd Regiment had been in Dutch pay since 1814; the 1st Regiment (which formed the real Nassau contingent) had only arrived a few days previously and had not yet been allotted to a Corps. Until the 16th it lay dispersed in cantonements between Brussels and Lowen.

'The 1st Regiment consisted of three battalions (until August 1814 both regiments had only had 2 battalions, and at this time were reinforced by men from the then disbanded 3rd Nassau Infantry Regiment).

'Each battalion had six companies, namely, 1 grenadier, 4 Jäger and 1 Flanquer company. The grenadiers formed on the right wing (of the battalion). The Flanquers on the left wing.

'Each company had 3 officers and 160 N.C.O.s and men. The battalion thus had 18 company officers and 960 N.C.O.s and men, the battalion headquarters had 13 officers and 40 N.C.O.s and men.

'This regiment, which until then formed my entire brigade, marched out of its camps early on the 16th and went to Quatre-Bras which they reached on the evening of the fight.

'On the 18th the Brigade, without being attached to any division, was ordered to join the First Army Corps commanded by H.R.H. the Prince of Oranien.

'The 2nd Regiment had 3 battalions each of 6 companies as for the 1st Regiment but each company had 4 officers and 150 N.C.O.s and men. Thus the Regiment had 24 officers and 900 N.C.O.s and men in the companies and 12 officers and 33 N.C.O.s and men in the regimental headquarters.

The Oldenburg Infantry Regiment in 1815. After being liberated from the French yoke in 1813, Oldenburg raised another line infantry regiment and a Landwehr force for service with the Allies against Napoleon. All military necessities were in short supply, so it cannot be assumed that the regiments which fought in the 1813 campaign appeared in perfect regulation dress; it was a case of 'come as you are', and many Prussian Landwehr regiments fought for months with a high proportion of men barefoot. Prussian influence can be seen again in the cut of the uniforms shown here, but, as with many north German regiments, the Oldenburgers used British Tower-marked Brown Bess muskets.

'This regiment, together with the Regiment Nassau–Oranien, formed the 2nd Brigade of the 2nd Royal Dutch Division.

'The former was commanded by Prinz Bernhard von Sachsen–Weimar, the latter was commanded by Generalleutnant von Perponcher. (The Regiment Oranien–Nassau, like the 2nd Nassau Regiment, had been taken into Dutch service for six years from 8 November 1814. Even so, the Regiment Oranien–Nassau also wore Dutch uniform. On 3 January 1816 the latter regiment was combined with the 1st Nassau Regiment and with the Prussian 35th Fusilier Regiment.)

'On 15 June 1815 the 2nd Battalion of the Dutch regiment Oranien–Nassau still carried French pattern muskets and each man had only ten cartridges. The Freiwillige Jäger had rifles of four different calibres and no more ammunition than the men of the 2nd Battalion.'

Uniform

'The grenadier companies had round bearskins (colpacks), all other companies wore shakos. The uniform of both regiments was dark green with black collar and cuffs and short skirts. The coat had a single row of yellow buttons on the front and the uniform, and the side pockets, were piped yellow. The breeches were dark green trimmed with yellow cord and the gaiters were black. Belts, bandoliers and pack straps were of buff leather.

'The uniform and headgear of the officers was as for that of the men, except that officers' coat-skirts were longer and they wore light grey and black striped pantaloons instead of green. All officers wore epaulettes which indicated their ranks and orange silk sashes. [*In Volume XVI, Plate 8 of Knotel's "Uniformkunde" there is a representation of the Nassau infantry. The text to this plate states that the uniform was worn from 1814–33 but in 1814 the epaulettes of officers in the flank companies were replaced by red or yellow "Achselwülste"-wings.*] The Jäger companies wore on their shakos a ball-shaped woollen pompon with a small tuft above it. The colours varied by company as follows:

1st Company	–	yellow
2nd Company	–	white
3rd Company	–	light blue
4th Company	–	black

'Under the pompon (at the front, top centre of the shako) was a small leather cockade. In

Hougoumont, 18 June 1815 – a French assault is taken in flank by a British battalion. Although fiercely contested throughout the battle, the farm never fell into French hands. It was defended by an Anglo–German garrison including numbers of Nassauers. (*National Army Museum*)

summer white linen trousers were worn.

'The regimental and battalion commanders and the six mounted Adjutant-majors, wore colpacks; only the general staff, 4 officers, wore bicorns with white, drooping feather plumes. All mounted officers carried sabres.

'The flags, of which each battalion carried one, were of pale yellow silk with the ducal badge in the centre embroidered in blue silk. The staff tip was gilt and from it hung two golden tassels.

'It is correct that on the day of the battle of Waterloo the men of the 1st Regiment were wearing white covers on their shakos and pouches but I had these removed at about 3 pm as they gave the enemy artillery a good aiming point. The men of the 2nd Regiment had the same covers but in black waxed cloth.

'No mounted officer rode a distinctive horse during the battle; only I rode a Falbe [a light coloured horse].'

Strength of the 1st Nassau Infantry Regiment on 18 June before the battle

Headquarters

1 Colonel	3 Battalion surgeons
1 Oberstleutnant	1 Divisional surgeon
3 Majors	12 N.C.O.s
3 Adjutant majors	1 Corporal
1 Regimental surgeon	33 Soldiers

Hougoumont today, taken from the south – the direction taken by the assaulting French troops. The heavy nature of the ground can clearly be seen, and must have made the advance physically tiring as well as militarily perilous. (*Jac Weller photograph, courtesy National Army Museum*)

1st Battalion

6 Captains	67 Corporals
6 Oberleutnants	18 Musicians
6 Unterleutnants	801 Soldiers
47 N.C.O.s	

The 2nd Battalion and the Landwehr Battalion had almost exactly the same strength and the whole regiment had 61 officers and approximately 2,840 men.

Strength of the 2nd Nassau Regiment on 16 June 1815 before the battle of Quatre-Bras

Headquarters

12 Officers	33 N.C.O.s and men

1st Battalion

23 Officers	847 N.C.O.s and men

2nd Battalion

24 Officers	842 men

3rd Battalion

24 Officers	853 men

TOTAL 83 officers and 2,575 men

The Brussels–Genappe road, with the farm of La Haye Sainte – looking south, towards the line held by the French. Nassau troops took part in the heroic defence of this essential bastion of Wellington's line at Waterloo, which eventually fell through lack of ammunition. Its loss precipitated the crisis of the battle. (*Jac Weller photograph, courtesy National Army Museum*)

Losses of the 1st Regiment at Waterloo on 18 June 1815

Unit	*Dead*		*Wounded*		*Missing*		*Total*	
	Offrs	*Men*	*Offrs*	*Men*	*Offrs*	*Men*	*Offrs*	*Men*
Headquarters	—	2	3	—	—	1	3	3
1st Battalion	—	113	11	157	—	116	11	386
2nd Battalion	3	96	4	131	—	81	7	308
Landwehr Battalion	2	39	2	82	—	65	4	186
TOTALS	5	250	20	370	—	263	25	883

The 2nd Regiment also fought at Quatre-Bras and its losses there were:

Unit	*Dead*	*Wounded*
1st Battalion	3	40
2nd Battalion	10	20
3rd Battalion	1	32

At Waterloo they then lost:

Unit	*Dead*		*Wounded*		*Missing*		*Total*	
	Offrs	*Men*	*Offrs*	*Men*	*Offrs*	*Men*	*Offrs*	*Men*
Headquarters	—	2	—	—	—	—	—	2
1st Battalion	2	27	6	46	—	27	8	110
2nd Battalion	1	13	7	45	—	14	8	72
3rd Battalion	1	27	7	62	—	50	8	139
TOTALS	4	69	20	153	—	91	24	323

Source: *Staatsarchiv Wiesbaden, VIII Nassau, Kriegsdepartement Nr 532, 26–27.*

The Uniforms of Nassau's Troops 1803-1815

The four infantry battalions wore dark green, long-skirted coats with red facings, piping and turnbacks. In the tails were vertical pocket-flaps with four buttons and yellow laces. Initially there was one grenadier company per battalion (a Carabinier company in the 3rd Jäger Battalion) and three fusilier companies; the grenadiers wore red plumes and epaulettes, the others black plumes and dark green shoulder straps. The shade of the facing colour and the colour of the buttons varied from battalion to battalion as shown here:

	Facings	*Buttons*	*Belts*
1st Battalion	Bright red	Yellow	Buff
2nd Battalion	Brick red	Yellow	Buff
3rd Battalion	Light red	White	Black
4th Battalion	Dark red	White	Buff

	Parade breeches	*Waistcoats*
1st Battalion	Grey	White
2nd Battalion	Dark green	Grey
3rd Battalion	Grey	Dark green
4th Battalion	Grey	White

Other distinctions were the headgear; the 1st Battalion wore Bavarian style black-leather helmets with black crest, black plume (red for grenadiers) a brass grenade badge and brass fittings; the 2nd Battalion wore what seem to have been Prussian-style, black-felt shakos with a black leather top band (N.C.O.s and drummers had

La Haye Sainte isolated during one of the French cavalry attacks; British fire from the garrison and the 95th Rifles in support north of the farm badly mauled the right flanks of French cavalry charges. This view seems to look south from a point close to the cross-roads marking the centre of the British front line. Note French foot and guns in background, waiting to exploit the cavalry charges. (*National Army Museum*)

gold top bands according to rank), black cockade, white cords, black plume; the 3rd Battalion wore bicorns with black cockade, yellow pompon, white loop, button and cords and the 4th Battalion wore shakos as for the 2nd but light green in colour with yellow (gold for N.C.O.s) top band, black cockade, bottom band and peak, and yellow cords. The grenadiers of the 4th Battalion wore the black shako with copper grenade badge and red plume and cords as shown in the colour plates.

Until 1809 all officers wore bicorns with black cockade, and loop and button in the regimental colour.

Collar and cuffs of the jackets were edged in yellow piping and badges of rank were shown by gold or silver lace to cuffs or collar or both. N.C.O.s and officers carried sticks as signs of office and it may be assumed that at this time officers wore silk waist sashes (in orange?). From 28 October

1806 they also wore gilt sword knots.

Legwear was, for parades, close fitting breeches with side-stripes and thigh-knots in short black gaiters with black leather buttons; in summer, white trousers over short white gaiters. Officers wore black Hessian boots with gold trim and tassel.

The *Reitende Jäger* were dressed all in dark green with silver lace and buttons, black leatherwork, black-leather helmets, high-crowned, Bavarian style for officers, low-crowned for other ranks. The helmets had black crests and green plumes with white metal front plate, chin-scales, peak edging and side struts. Weapons were a carbine, pistols and a curved, light cavalry sabre in a steel sheath. Sabretasches were of black leather with the crowned cypher 'FA' and those of the officers had a broad silver edging.

In 1808, when the infantry was reorganised, the uniforms were also altered. The helmets of the old 1st Battalion (von Todenwarth) were given to the first grenadier companies of the two new regiments, the second grenadier companies wore French style grenadier shakos. By 1810 all grenadiers should have been issued with the brown fur colpack with red bag, pompon, plume

Nassau Infantry flag, 1806–15. Of pale yellow cloth, it bore a light blue shield, a gold and red crown, and a laurel wreath in green with a gold ribbon. The shield was charged with a gold lion with red tongue and claws, and with gold vertical bars. The brown staff had a gold spearhead, nails and cords.

trousers had yellow side-stripes and thigh-knots.

On 15 October 1807 French muskets and sabres were issued to replace the old-fashioned and worn-out weapons which the Nassauers previously had and French badges of rank and service were introduced. For other ranks these consisted of diagonal stripes across both lower sleeves:

Corporal	two red stripes
Sergeant	one gold stripe edged red
Company Quartermaster	two red stripes (and two gold chevrons on the upper sleeve)
Sergeant Major	two gold stripes edged red.

Service badges were also after the French pattern and took the form of yellow chevrons, point up, on the upper left sleeve.

Officers wore gilt gorgets and gold sword knots and their rank was indicated by gold epaulettes on the shoulders:

Lieutenant	fringed epaulette right; contre-epaulette left
Premier Lieutenant	fringed epaulette left; contre-epaulette right
Hauptmann	two fringed epaulettes
Major	two epaulettes with silver straps and gold bullion fringes
Oberstleutnant	two golden epaulettes, only the left with bullion fringes
Oberst	two golden epaulettes with gold bullion fringes

Officers wore gold shako cords on parade.

The cavalry uniform changed little at this time except that the helmets gave way to black fur colpacks with dark green bag (officers with silver tassel, the men with white). Dark green pelisses with black fur and white lace and buttons were added, and the expensive, close fitting dark-green breeches in hussar boots gave way to dark-green overalls with black leather fittings. Badges of rank were a series of white (silver for officers) chevrons situated over the cuff.

and cords shown in the colour plates. The élite companies (grenadier and the newly raised Voltigeur) wore French style distinctions: grenadiers – red hat-trim, red epaulettes and red sabre-strap, red grenade-badge in the turnbacks; voltigeurs, green plume with yellow tip, brass horn shako-badge, green cords, green epaulettes and sabre strap, yellow-horn badges in the turnbacks. Fusiliers wore shakos with white cords, black cockade, company colour pompon (1st Company – yellow, 2nd – white, 3rd – light blue, 4th – black) and a badge in the shape of a brass oval bearing the regimental number, surrounded by a trophy of arms and flags.

The jacket remained dark green but facings became black, buttons yellow, turnbacks green, edged yellow, waistcoats initially white, later dark green with yellow piping, legwear either grey breeches in black gaiters as before or, later, dark green trousers over short black gaiters. The

The Plates

NASSAU

A1 Private, 1st Battalion, summer dress, 1803
This battalion was also known as the 'Leib-Bataillon' (Life Battalion), a commonly used title on the Continent for the most senior regiment, battalion, company or squadron. It was also the custom to name units after their commanders and thus the 1st Battalion was also known as the 'Bataillon von Todenwarth'. The boiled-leather helmet is very similar to that worn at this time by the Bavarian army. The front badge was a flaming grenade in brass; the grenadiers wore a red plume at the side of their helmets, the musketeers the black one shown here. For winter wear the men wore grey trousers with black thigh-knots and side-stripes and black gaiters to below the knee, the gaiters over the trousers. The coat was single-breasted and cut away in an oval shape at the bottom so that the white waistcoat showed. The coat was edged in red piping. The pouch plate bears the lion of Nassau.

A2 Drummer, 2nd Battalion, summer capaign dress, 1806
Here the new yellow shako trim is shown; the Nassau drummers did not wear reversed colours but were distinguished by the yellow lace on their chests and the yellow chevrons on their arms. The 1st and 2nd Battalions wore buff leatherwork, the 3rd (Rifle) Battalion wore black. The brass drum was the modern design and much lighter to carry than the older, bigger wooden models; this was important as the drummers were usually boys of about thirteen to sixteen years of age.

A3 Fusiliers, 4th Battalion, summer campaign dress, 1806
This battalion was recruited mainly from the Weilburg area of the duchy and was also known by the name of its commander – Major von Kruse. In November 1806 the black shako shown here was brightened up with a yellow top band, pompon and cords. The black plume was added for parades. Note the rather unusual soldiers' coats

Lieutenant-General Friedrich Christian Dietrich von Preen, who commanded the 3rd (Landwehr) Battalion of the 1st Nassau Infantry Regiment at Waterloo and was badly wounded in the neck during an attempt to relieve La Haye Sainte. Born in Waldeck in 1787, he fought as an officer in the service of that principality in Dutch pay until 1809. As a lieutenant in the 3rd Dutch Infantry Regiment in Spain, he transferred in March of that year to the Nassau service, retaining his rank in the 2nd Nassau Infantry Regiment. He served as A.D.C. to General von Schäffer, returning with him to Nassau and later rejoining his troops with a reinforcement draft. In 1813 he was named a knight of the Legion of Honour. On 25 October 1813 he was promoted major. It was von Preen who carried his Duke's secret verbal orders to von Kruse, instructing him to take his regiment over to the British. In 1814 von Preen was given the task of organising Nassau's Landwehr. His bravery at Waterloo brought him the Willems-Order and a presentation sabre. He retired in 1848 and died in 1856. His uniform here – that of his final rank – is dark green faced with black velvet, and has gold embroidery and epaulettes.

with long skirts to the knee; this custom was normally reserved for officers. The green breeches shown here were parade wear; normal legwear was grey breeches in the short gaiters. It was in this uniform that the Nassauers took the field in 1806 to help Napoleon crush Prussia.

B1 Fusilier, 2nd Battalion, parade dress, 1806
The origin of the green shako shown here is not known. The green coat was as for the other battalions but the facings were dark red compared with the medium red of the 1st and 2nd Battalions. The dark green plume was put on for parades and when taking part in a prepared battle. For winter

The Prince of Orange is wounded during the latter stages of the Battle of Waterloo. Though undoubtedly a young man of courage and dash, the Prince was not a great asset to the Anglo–Netherlands army in 1815. Throughout the two battles of Quatre-Bras and Waterloo he continually brought the full weight of his negligible military experience to bear upon his hapless subordinates, with fatal results for hundreds of them. His speciality was ordering troops safely established in squares to deploy into line in the face of enemy cavalry, a course of action which must have endeared him to Marshal Ney. At last, in the later stages of the fighting on 18 June, a providential musket ball in the shoulder removed him from the scene, just in time to save the 1st Nassau Infantry from suffering the same fate. (**National Army Museum**)

wear grey breeches with black thigh-knots and side-stripes were worn inside short black gaiters. The back of the jacket had red turnbacks and vertical pocket flaps each with four buttons and yellow button hole laces; two large buttons were in the small of the back. Hair was worn powdered and queued until 1806–7. Commander of this battalion was Major von Holbach, and the unit was recruited from the area of Usingen.

B2 Grenadier Sergeant, 4th Battalion, winter parade dress, 1806

This company of the battalion wore black shakos which appear to have been of the then-current Prussian model with a copper grenade badge under the black cockade. The huge red horsehair plume is interesting as both Russia and Prussia introduced plumes of this pattern into their armies in the period 1809–15. The other grenadier hallmarks were of very French flavour – red shako cords, red woollen epaulettes and red sabre fist-strap. Additionally, they wore gaiters with red trim and tassel to the tops. As in most Continental armies, the packs were made of calfskin whereas in the British army they were of canvas painted in the facing colour of the regiment.

B3 Rifleman, 3rd Battalion, summer parade dress, 1806

During November 1806 the battalion began to receive the new pattern shakos as worn by the 2nd Battalion but it is likely that only a fraction of the men had them during the campaign period. The red facings of the 3rd Battalion were slightly lighter in colour than those of the 2nd Battalion.

Wellington signals the general advance at the close of the Battle of Waterloo. (*National Army Museum*)

Being riflemen they were armed (at least in part) with rifles carried in the traditional huntsman's manner. Their equipment was also different from that of their comrades; instead of an ammunition pouch and pack, they wore small cartridge pouches on the front of their belts and carried their other kit in a black leather satchel or 'Ranzentasche'. Another variation of the uniform was the orange thigh-knots on the grey breeches. Instead of a sabre, the riflemen carried a straight-bladed sword-bayonet with a green fist strap.

C Nassau: Officers, Reitende Jäger, parade dress, 1807

Until 1809 the *Reitende Jäger* (Chasseurs à Cheval) wore the helmets shown in this plate; thereafter the black fur busby seems to have been adopted. Officers' helmets were of the same pattern as then worn by officers of Bavarian Chevau-légers with the following differences: the dark green plume was worn on the right-hand side of the helmet whereas the Bavarians wore a white plume on the left and the oval front plate bore the cypher 'FA' (Friedrich August, Duke of Nassau) instead of the Bavarian 'MJK' (Maximilian Joseph, König). Other ranks' helmets were very similar in appearance to those of the officers but were considerably lower in the crown; their crests were of black sheepskin over a stuffed 'sausage' instead of the bearskin of the officers. Knötel, in his Plate 34 of Volume V of his *Uniformenkunde – Lose Blätter*, shows both officers and other ranks as having five rows of white metal buttons on the chests of their dolmans. This is most unusual and it was more conventional for other ranks to have only three such rows. Some authorities state that each dolman had fifteen rows of white (silver for officers) lace across the chest but the actual number worn may well have depended upon the wearer's size! As in the French light cavalry, an officer's rank was indicated by the number and width of the bands of silver (or gold) embroidery to be seen

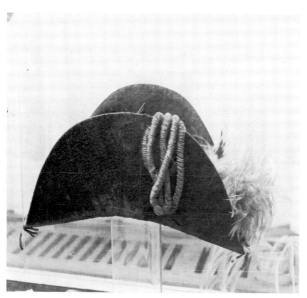

The bicorne supposedly worn by Marshal Blücher at Ligny and Waterloo, typical of the headgear of senior and staff officers of all the armies of the day. It is now in the Museum for German History on the Unter den Linden in East Berlin. The rather sadly drooping plume obscures the black feathers at its base.

A serpent, an odd but aptly named musical instrument carried by many military bands in Napoleon's day. This example hangs in the Bavarian fortress of Coburg.

above the cuff and around the thigh knots. The cypher 'FA' on the sabretasche is often wrongly reproduced as 'FM' by artists who copy the old paintings without sufficient knowledge of who sat on the ducal throne at which time. Saddles were of the wooden 'Bock' style, as produced in Turkey and Hungary hundreds of years ago, and harness was of the light cavalry pattern and, for officers, was decorated with tiny white cowrie shells.

D1   Pioneer, 1st Infantry Regiment, 1809–13
Sappers (one per company) wore grenadier appointments (red epaulettes, busby with red bag, cords, pompon and plume), full beards, and the aprons, gauntlets and arm badges shown here. Their armament consisted of a sabre with red fist-strap, carbine (usually carried slung over the shoulder) and a heavy axe for clearing obstacles.

D2   Officer, Reitende Jäger, 1810 (in Spain)
Evidence tends to show that only officers wore the bright red and rather baggy breeches shown here; other ranks wore the previously mentioned grey overalls with a dark green side-piping and white buttons. The old helmets have now given way to brown busbies with dark green bags and white (silver) tassels. Other changes in the uniform are that hussar pattern, dark green pelisses with brown fur and silver lace and buttons have been adopted and the silver pouch belt has given way to a black one, edged in silver and with silver picker equipment.

Supplies of clothing scarcely ever reached any of the men serving in Napoleon's armies in Spain (or in any other of his campaigns come to that!) so the troops were forced to make do as best they could. This often meant that each battalion would buy (or steal) cloth in the area in which they were quartered and would have their tailors make it up into clothing on the spot.

It seems that Spain was richly endowed with Franciscan abbeys at this period as many contemporary diaries and paintings show French and allied soldiers in brown trousers and greatcoats during these campaigns. It is an interesting fact that Wellington's troops scarcely ever suffered logistical disasters or shortages on the scale that Napoleon inflicted on his men.

D3 Trooper, Reitende Jäger, parade dress, 1806
This is the uniform worn by the 'Green Hunters' (as they were nicknamed) in the campaign of 1806 against Prussia when the unit went to Berlin. It is likely that on campaign the decorated green breeches would have been covered (or replaced) by much cheaper and more comfortable grey overalls buttoning up the outsides of the legs.

E1 Officer (Premierleutnant) of voltigeurs, parade dress, 1810
The old-fashioned bicorn was replaced by the shako for officers of fusilier and voltigeur companies in about 1810. Grenadier officers then adopted the busby worn by their men. Officers' shakos had gold cords, front plate and chin-scales and vari-coloured tufted pompons according to company (fusiliers – yellow, white, light blue or black; voltigeurs dark green). Sign of office (from 1806 on) was the gilt gorget with a circular central silver plate, bearing the crowned cypher 'FA'(?) and the gold sword knot. Rank was indicated by gold epaulettes exactly as in the French Napoleonic army. The buff baldric had a gold oval plate with the lion of Nassau on it.

E2 Voltigeur Corporal, campaign dress, 1809–13
The voltigeur distinctions are almost identical with those used in the French Napoleonic army, i.e. green plume with a yellow tip, green cords and pompon, green woollen epaulettes and sabre fist-strap. Turnback badges in the shape of yellow hunting horns were worn and the ammunition pouch badge was also a distinction. Fusiliers had neither turnback badges nor pouch badges. Grenadiers had red grenades on their turnbacks and a brass grenade on their pouches. Both Nassau infantry regiments had black facings since 1808; in 1809 the orange decoration to collar and cuffs was replaced by a plain yellow edging as shown here.

E3 Drummer of Fusiliers, 2nd Infantry Regiment, 1809–13
The shakos now worn by the fusiliers and voltigeurs of the Nassau infantry would seem to be of French issue pattern. The old drummer's distinctions have been retained.

F1 Oldenburg: Corporal, Voltigeur Company, 1808–11
After joining the Rheinbund on 14 October 1808, the Duchy of Oldenburg existed until 13 December 1810 when it was dissolved by Napoleon and incorporated into Metropolitan France. The uniform shown here is a mixture of Prussian, Austrian and French styles; the four fusilier and the voltigeur companies of the battalion wore Austrian 'Jäger' pattern hats (the fusiliers with a white plume, the voltigeurs dark green), while the grenadiers wore black bearskins with a red top patch – certainly a little French influence. The coat, with its twin rows of buttons, is very Prussian. The regimental history shows an N.C.O. with the silver stripe on his upper arm; this is not confirmed in any other source. Officers wore the hats of their companies but with a long plume following the top of the upturned brim with the bushy end to the rear. These plumes were white with a red tip. The sign of office was a silver gorget with gold badge and a silver aiguilette on the right shoulder. Officers carried curved sabres in black and gold sheaths on silver slings from a silver waistbelt worn over the coat. They wore white breeches in straight-topped black boots; their coat-skirts reached to knee level.

F2 Nassau: Sergeant-major of Grenadiers, 1st Regiment, 1815
This plate shows the uniform worn by the Nassauers at Quatre-Bras and Waterloo. The French-style epaulettes in red and green for the élite companies (grenadiers and voltigeurs) have now been replaced by 'Achselwülste' or shoulder rolls designed originally to prevent a hunter's slung rifle from slipping off his shoulder. The grenadiers' Achselwülste were red, the voltigeurs' yellow. Voltigeurs now wore a brass hunting horn on their shakos and had green cords, pompon, plume and sabre-strap.

F3 Oldenburg: Drummer, Grenadier Company, Drill order
As in many other armies of the day, Oldenburg employed Negroes for its regimental band (at least for the grenadier company). Drummers' badges were the red and white 'swallows' nests' at the tops of the sleeves and the four red and white

The Oldenburg Infantry Regiment in 1848; many German regiments traced their lineage directly from the Napoleonic era to the First World War, and those which took on the traditions of the King's German Legion bore British Peninsular battle-honours in 1914. The Oldenburgers of 1848 still wore dark blue faced red with white shoulder-straps; the helmet, though a close copy of the current Prussian model, has a rather individual type of peak and spike.

chevrons on each arm. The swallows' nests were edged with red and white fringes along the bottoms. Officers' bearskins had silver cords.

OLDENBURG

G1   Fusilier sergeant, 129th 'French' Line Infantry Regiment, 1812

The men of the old Regiment Oldenburg were sent to Osnabrück in 1811 to form part of the newly-raised '*129ᵉ de Ligne*'. The uniform shown here is completely French. Grenadiers had red shako-cords and plumes, red epaulettes and red sabre-knots; voltigeurs, yellow over green plumes, green cords, green epaulettes and green sabre-straps. Drill and discipline were also French, which meant that corporal punishment was not used. Officers had gold shako-cords, wore gold gorgets, and carried straight bladed swords on

waistbelts worn over the waistcoat and under the coat. Napoleon commanded that these new regiments should not receive their eagles until they had proved themselves in battle – the Russian campaign gave liberal opportunities for the issue of many eagles, unfortunately the casualties were so heavy that by the end of 1812 there were often too few men left in a regiment to carry the colours!

G2   Officer, Regiment Oldenburg, winter parade dress, 1814

The Prussian influence in this uniform has now completely ousted the Austrian and French touches which were seen prior to 1811. The shako plate bears a 'P', the initial of the then-reigning Duke of Oldenburg, Peter Friedrich Ludwig. As was fashionable in Prussia in those days, the uniforms were very closely cut and the sleeves were so long that the bottom button of the cuff flap was often worn open to give the hand a little more freedom and to stop the sleeve from creasing too much. The plumes of the men were slightly shorter and thicker than those of the officers and the mens' shako plates and crowns were of brass. Drummers had red swallows nests as before, edged in white, but no chevrons on the sleeves. It seems that all companies were composed of musketeers and that there were no grenadier or light companies. The shako shown in the regimental history would seem to have been of the then-current Prussian model.

G3 Private, Freiwillige Jäger Detachment of the Regiment Oldenburg, field dress, 1814
On 27 November 1813 Oldenburg finally shook off the French yoke and formed one battalion of line infantry (1st Battalion) and one battalion of Landwehr infantry (2nd Battalion) which together constituted the 'Regiment Oldenburg'. Attached to the 2nd Battalion was a detachment of *'Freiwillige Jäger'* ('Volunteer hunters') or Gentlemen Rankers. These volunteers had to be rich enough to clothe and equip themselves and were addressed by officers and N.C.O.s as 'Sie' (the polite form) instead of the usual 'Du' (familiar form) which was used to the common soldiers. The *Freiwillige Jägers* were armed with rifles and sword-bayonets and their facings were dark green instead of the red of the rest of the battalion. They were used for skirmishing duties, and wore the Landwehr cross in silver on their caps, as did the Prussian Landwehr. Their belts were black whereas the rest of the 2nd Battalion wore white.

NASSAU

H1 Jäger, 1st Infantry Regiment, 1815 (at Waterloo)
This figure is shown wearing the white shako cover and white pouch cover which their commander, Oberst von Kruse, ordered them to re-

Helmet of an Other Rank, Oldenburg Infantry Regiment Nr. 91, 1914, now in the military museum in the castle of Rastatt in Baden. Local feeling survived in many parts of Germany long after Prussia welded the previously independent states into a single nation in the 1870s; even today there is strong anti-Prussian feeling in Hanover and Bavaria. This regiment continued to recruit in Oldenburg, and its helmet bears the old badge of the crowned ducal crest on an eight-pointed star.

move at about 3 pm on the day of Waterloo as they were too conspicuous a target for the French artillery. Badges of rank were still French but the epaulettes of the élite companies had given way to shoulder rolls. Belts were of buff leather and packs were of calfskin as they had previously been. The shako plate was brass and as for the figure of the drummer in Plate E1.

H2 Officer of the General Staff, parade dress, 1815
This small corps of four officers kept alive the newly founded traditions of the general staff – a body of officers designed to help a commander

An interesting link with the Nassauers of Spain and Waterloo; note the similarity between this badge and the central device of the Nassau colours. It is the patch worn on the upper left arm by present-day members of the German Bundeswehr's 5th Panzer Division, garrisoned in the area of the old Duchy of Nassau. The blue shield with its yellow lion and bars is worn with different coloured edges to indicate sub-unit. Divisional troops have black and white striped edges; 13th Panzer-Grenadier Brigade has white edges; 14th Panzer Brigade has red edges, and 15th Panzer Brigade yellow edges. This colour code by seniority (white, red, yellow, and where applicable blue) is the same as that used in the Prussian army of 1813.

manage his forces and win his battles. On field service the expensive white breeches would be covered by grey overalls with a row of buttons down the outside of each leg. These four officers (and the commander) were the only Nassau officers to wear bicorns, the rest of the regimental officers wore brown fur colpacks like the grenadiers.

H3   Officer of Grenadiers, 1st Infantry Regiment, 1815
The regimental history states that officers wore gold epaulettes to indicate their rank in 1813 and this is confirmed by General von Kruse's letter on that campaign. Knötel, in the text to his Plate 8 of Volume XVI of his *Uniformenkunde*, states that in 1814 the epaulettes of the officers in the grenadier and 'flanquer' companies were replaced by red or yellow *Achselwülste* or wings in the style of those worn by the officers of British light companies. Page 111 of the Regimental

History states that 'the epaulettes for the men were discarded', but does not clarify the position of these items for officers. Being a company officer, this man carries a straight bladed *Degen* on a buff baldric; mounted officers carried curved sabres on black and silver slings.

SOURCES

Bernays, *Schicksale des Grossherzogthums Frankfurt*
Knötel, *Uniformenkunde – Lose Blätter, Vol. V*
Knötel, *Uniformkunde, Vol. XVI*
Weiland, *Darstellung der Kaiserlich Französischen Armee 1812*

National Army Museum, London
Staatsarchiv Wiesbaden, VIII Nassau, Kriegsdepartement Nr 532, 26–27